MW01241628

BRUSSELS
RESTAURANT GUIDE

RESTAURANTS, BARS AND CAFES
Your Guide to Authentic Regional Eats

BRUSSELS RESTAURANT GUIDE 2022
Best Rated Restaurants in Brussels, Belgium

© Ralph H. Steinbeck
© E.G.P. Editorial

Printed in USA.

ISBN-13: 9798749977080

BRUSSELS RESTAURANT GUIDE

The Most Recommended Restaurants in Brussels

This directory is dedicated to the Business Owners and Managers who provide the experience that the locals and tourists enjoy. Thanks you very much for all that you do and thank for being the "People Choice".

Thanks to everyone that posts their reviews online and the amazing reviews sites that make our life easier.

The places listed in this book are the most positively reviewed and recommended by locals and travelers from around the world.

Thank you for your time and enjoy the directory that is designed with locals and tourist in mind!

TOP 500
RESTAURANTS
Ranked from #1 to #500

#1
Noordzee - Mer du Nord
Cuisines: Seafood, Fish & Chips
Average price: Modest
Area: Bruxelles, Centre-Ville
Address: Rue Sainte Catherine 45
1000 Brussels, Belgium
Phone: 02 513 11 92

#2
My Little Cup
Cuisines: Coffee & Tea, Breakfast & Brunch
Average price: Modest
Area: Bruxelles, Centre-Ville
Address: Rue de la Croix de Fer 53
1000 Brussels, Belgium
Phone: 0483 01 56 60

#3
Nuetnigenough
Cuisines: Belgian
Average price: Modest
Area: Bruxelles, Centre-Ville, Stalingrad
Address: Rue du Lombard 25
1000 Brussels, Belgium
Phone: 02 513 78 84

#4
BELI
Cuisines: Lebanese, Cafe,
Breakfast & Brunch
Average price: Modest
Area: Bruxelles, Centre-Ville, Marolles
Address: Rue Joseph Stevens 11
1000 Brussels, Belgium
Phone: 02 538 88 88

#5
Pré de Chez Nous
Cuisines: Belgian
Average price: Modest
Area: Bruxelles, Centre-Ville
Address: Rue des Dominicains 19
1000 Brussels, Belgium
Phone: 02 833 37 37

#6
Thiên Long
Cuisines: Vietnamese
Average price: Modest
Area: Bruxelles, Centre-Ville, Dansaert
Address: rue Van Artevelde 12
1000 Brussels, Belgium
Phone: 02 511 34 80

#7
Pasta Divina
Cuisines: Italian
Average price: Modest
Area: Bruxelles, Centre-Ville
Address: Rue de la Montagne 16
1000 Brussels, Belgium
Phone: 02 511 21 55

#8
Winehouse Osteria
Cuisines: Italian, Wine Bar
Average price: Modest
Area: Bruxelles, Centre-Ville, Anneesens
Address: Rue de la Grande Ile 42
1000 Brussels, Belgium
Phone: 02 350 09 21

#9
Rachel
Cuisines: Bagels, Burgers, Belgian
Average price: Modest
Area: Bruxelles, Centre-Ville, Stalingrad
Address: Rue du Marché au Charbon 100
1000 Brussels, Belgium
Phone: 02 503 37 59

#10
Tonton Garby
Cuisines: Fast Food, Sandwiches
Average price: Inexpensive
Area: Bruxelles, Centre-Ville, Quartier Royal
Address: Rue Duquesnoy 6
1000 Brussels, Belgium
Phone: 0484 29 02 16

#11
La Clef d'Or
Cuisines: Belgian, Cafe
Average price: Modest
Area: Bruxelles, Centre-Ville, Marolles
Address: Place du Jeu de Balle 1
1000 Brussels, Belgium
Phone: 02 511 97 62

#12
Le Poechenellekelder
Cuisines: Beer Bar, Tapas/Small Plates
Average price: Modest
Area: Bruxelles, Centre-Ville, Stalingrad
Address: Rue du Chêne 5
1000 Brussels, Belgium
Phone: 02 511 92 62

#13
Viva M'Boma
Cuisines: Belgian
Average price: Expensive
Area: Bruxelles, Centre-Ville
Address: Rue de Flandre 17
1000 Brussels, Belgium
Phone: 02 512 15 93

#14
Jour de Fête
Cuisines: French
Average price: Modest
Area: Bruxelles, Centre-Ville, Anneesens
Address: Boulevard Anspach 181
1000 Brussels, Belgium
Phone: 02 512 38 00

#15
Knees to Chin
Cuisines: Asian Fusion
Average price: Modest
Area: Bruxelles, Centre-Ville, Dansaert
Address: rue de Flandre 28
1000 Brussels, Belgium
Phone: 02 503 18 31

#16
Le Seventy-Five
Cuisines: Wine Bar, Burgers, Cocktail Bar
Average price: Modest
Area: Bruxelles, Centre-Ville, Stalingrad
Address: Rue des Alexiens 75
1000 Brussels, Belgium
Phone: 0499 63 38 78

#17
Peï & Meï
Cuisines: Belgian
Average price: Expensive
Area: Bruxelles, Centre-Ville, Marolles
Address: Rue de Rollebeek 15
1000 Brussels, Belgium
Phone: 02 880 53 39

#18
Houtsiplou
Cuisines: Belgian, Brasserie, Steakhouse
Average price: Modest
Area: Bruxelles, Centre-Ville, Stalingrad
Address: Place Rouppe 9
1000 Brussels, Belgium
Phone: 02 511 38 16

#19
C'est Bon C'est Belge - Le Cellier
Cuisines: Belgian
Average price: Modest
Area: Bruxelles, Centre-Ville, Stalingrad
Address: Rue du Bon-Secours 14-16
1000 Brussels, Belgium
Phone: 02 512 19 99

#20
Les Filles
Cuisines: European, Delicatessen,
Breakfast & Brunch
Average price: Modest
Area: Bruxelles, Centre-Ville, Dansaert
Address: Rue du Vieux Marché aux Grains
46, 1000 Brussels, Belgium
Phone: 02 534 04 83

#21
Le Cirio
Cuisines: Brasserie, Lounge
Average price: Modest
Area: Bruxelles, Centre-Ville, Dansaert
Address: Rue de la Bourse 18
1000 Brussels, Belgium
Phone: 02 512 13 95

#22
Selecto
Cuisines: Brasserie, European
Average price: Exclusive
Area: Bruxelles, Centre-Ville
Address: Rue de Flandre 95
1000 Brussels, Belgium
Phone: 02 511 40 95

#23
Makisu
Cuisines: Japanese, Sushi Bar
Average price: Modest
Area: Bruxelles, Centre-Ville, Dansaert
Address: Rue de Flandre 6
1000 Brussels, Belgium
Phone: 02 513 81 31

#24
Le Fontainas
Cuisines: Cafe
Average price: Modest
Area: Bruxelles, Centre-Ville, Stalingrad
Address: Rue du Marché au Charbon 91
1000 Brussels, Belgium
Phone: 02 503 31 12

#25
Balls & Glory Brussels Bourse
Cuisines: Belgian
Average price: Modest
Area: Bruxelles, Centre-Ville, Dansaert
Address: Rue Henri Maus, 35
1000 Brussels, Belgium
Phone: 02 513 37 87

#26
Le Mangeoire
Cuisines: Cafe, Delicatessen
Average price: Modest
Area: Bruxelles, Centre-Ville
Address: Rue du Congrès 34
1000 Brussels, Belgium
Phone: 02 223 00 02

#27
Alexandre
Cuisines: European
Average price: Exclusive
Area: Bruxelles, Centre-Ville, Stalingrad
Address: Rue du Midi 164
1000 Brussels, Belgium
Phone: 02 502 40 55

#28
Beaucoup Fish
Cuisines: Seafood, Delicatessen
Average price: Expensive
Area: Bruxelles, Centre-Ville
Address: Rue Van Gaver 2
1000 Brussels, Belgium
Phone: 02 218 64 20

#29
Al Jannah
Cuisines: Lebanese
Average price: Modest
Area: Bruxelles, Centre-Ville, Marolles
Address: Rue Blaes 59
1000 Brussels, Belgium
Phone: 02 514 08 44

#30
Comme Chez Soi
Cuisines: European, Belgian
Average price: Exclusive
Area: Bruxelles, Centre-Ville, Stalingrad
Address: Place Rouppe 23
1000 Brussels, Belgium
Phone: 02 512 29 21

#31
Boulangerie Charli
Cuisines: Bakery, Sandwiches
Average price: Modest
Area: Bruxelles, Centre-Ville, Dansaert
Address: Rue Sainte-Catherine 34
1000 Brussels, Belgium
Phone: 02 513 63 32

#33
Jat' Café
Cuisines: Juice Bar, Breakfast & Brunch
Average price: Modest
Area: Bruxelles, Centre-Ville, Quartier Royal
Address: Rue de Namur 28
1000 Brussels, Belgium
Phone: 02 503 03 32

#32
Osteria A l'Ombra
Cuisines: Italian
Average price: Modest
Area: Bruxelles, Centre-Ville, Grand-Place
Address: Rue des Harengs 2
1000 Brussels, Belgium
Phone: 02 511 67 10

#34
FORK
Cuisines: Concept Shop, Bistro,
Venue & Event Space
Average price: Modest
Area: Bruxelles, Centre-Ville, Dansaert
Address: Rue Du Rempart Des Moines 13
1000 Brussels, Belgium
Phone: 02 201 77 70

#35
Henri & Agnes
Cuisines: Health Market,
Breakfast & Brunch, Caterer
Average price: Modest
Area: Bruxelles, Quartier Européen
Address: Rue Véronèse 48
1000 Brussels, Belgium
Phone: 0471 22 28 02

#36
Strofilia
Cuisines: Greek
Average price: Modest
Area: Bruxelles, Centre-Ville
Address: Rue du Marché aux Porcs 11-13
1000 Brussels, Belgium
Phone: 02 512 32 93

#37
Vincent
Cuisines: Belgian, Barbeque, Seafood
Average price: Expensive
Area: Bruxelles, Centre-Ville
Address: Rue des Dominicains 8-10
1000 Brussels, Belgium
Phone: 02 511 26 07

#38
La Guinguette en Ville
Cuisines: Belgian
Average price: Expensive
Area: Bruxelles, Centre-Ville
Address: Place du Béguinage 9
1000 Brussels, Belgium
Phone: 02 229 02 22

#39
Le Petit Boxeur
Cuisines: Belgian, French
Average price: Expensive
Area: Bruxelles, Centre-Ville, Dansaert
Address: Rue Borgval 3
1000 Brussels, Belgium
Phone: 02 511 40 00

#40
Knees To Chin
Cuisines: Asian Fusion
Average price: Modest
Area: Ixelles, Chatelain
Address: Rue de Livourne 125
1000 Brussels, Belgium
Phone: 02 644 18 11

#41
Café Velvet
Cuisines: Breakfast & Brunch, Cafe
Average price: Inexpensive
Area: Bruxelles, Centre-Ville
Address: Quai au Bois à Brûler 27
1000 Brussels, Belgium
Phone: 02 217 80 91

#42
Monk
Cuisines: Cafe
Average price: Modest
Area: Bruxelles, Centre-Ville
Address: Rue Sainte Catherine 42
1000 Brussels, Belgium
Phone: 02 511 75 11

#43
Lola
Cuisines: Brasserie
Average price: Exclusive
Area: Bruxelles, Centre-Ville, Sablon
Address: Place du Grand Sablon 33
1000 Brussels, Belgium
Phone: 02 514 24 60

#44
Publico
Cuisines: Mediterranean
Average price: Modest
Area: Bruxelles, Centre-Ville, Dansaert
Address: Rue des Chartreux 32
1000 Brussels, Belgium
Phone: 02 503 04 30

#45
Comptoir des Galeries
Cuisines: Brasserie, Belgian
Average price: Expensive
Area: Bruxelles, Centre-Ville
Address: Galerie du Roi 6
1000 Brussels, Belgium
Phone: 02 213 74 74

#46
Gazzetta
Cuisines: Wine Bar, Italian
Average price: Modest
Area: Ixelles, Bruxelles, Louise
Address: Rue de la Longue Haie 12
1050 Brussels, Belgium
Phone: 02 513 92 13

#47
Les Gens que J'aime
Cuisines: Bar, Cafe, French
Average price: Modest
Area: Bruxelles, Centre-Ville, Dansaert
Address: Rue du Midi 15
1000 Brussels, Belgium
Phone: 02 523 28 76

#48
G Spud
Cuisines: Salad, Breakfast & Brunch
Average price: Inexpensive
Area: Saint-Gilles, Louise
Address: Rue Jourdan 9
1060 Brussels, Belgium
Phone: 02 538 05 08

#49
Sakagura
Cuisines: Japanese
Average price: Modest
Area: Bruxelles, Centre-Ville, Martyrs
Address: Rue du Marais 15
1000 Brussels, Belgium
Phone: 02 201 78 88

#50
Aux Armes de Bruxelles
Cuisines: Belgian
Average price: Expensive
Area: Bruxelles, Centre-Ville, Grand-Place
Address: Rue des Bouchers 13
1000 Brussels, Belgium
Phone: 02 511 55 50

#51
Ajiyoshi
Cuisines: Japanese, Sushi Bar
Average price: Expensive
Area: Bruxelles, Centre-Ville
Address: Quai aux Briques 32
1000 Brussels, Belgium
Phone: 02 502 02 98

#52
Le Funambule
Cuisines: Desserts, Waffles
Average price: Inexpensive
Area: Bruxelles, Centre-Ville, Stalingrad
Address: Rue de l'Etuve 42
1000 Brussels, Belgium
Phone: 0470 03 54 40

#53
Makisu
Cuisines: Japanese, Sushi Bar
Average price: Modest
Area: Ixelles, Bruxelles, Louise
Address: Rue du Bailli 5
1000 Brussels, Belgium
Phone: 02 640 45 50

#54
La Boussole
Cuisines: Brasserie, Seafood
Average price: Modest
Area: Bruxelles, Centre-Ville
Address: Quai au Bois à Brûler 61
1000 Brussels, Belgium
Phone: 02 218 58 77

#55
De Pistolei
Cuisines: Caterer, Sandwiches
Average price: Inexpensive
Area: Bruxelles, Centre-Ville, Quartier Royal
Address: Rue de la madeleine 5
1000 Brussels, Belgium
Phone: 02 502 95 02

#56
Ars Vinorum
Cuisines: Italian
Average price: Expensive
Area: Bruxelles, Porte De Namur, Centre-Ville, Quartier Royal
Address: Rue de la Reinette 6
1000 Brussels, Belgium
Phone: 02 503 39 33

#57
Aux Paves De Bruxelles
Cuisines: Cafe
Average price: Expensive
Area: Bruxelles, Centre-Ville, Grand-Place
Address: Rue du Marché aux Fromages 1
1000 Brussels, Belgium
Phone: 02 502 04 57

#58
C'est Bon C'est Belge
Cuisines: Belgian
Average price: Modest
Area: Bruxelles, Centre-Ville, Marolles
Address: Rue de Rollebeek 3-5
1000 Brussels, Belgium
Phone: 02 512 29 99

#59
Le Pré Salé
Cuisines: Belgian
Average price: Expensive
Area: Bruxelles, Centre-Ville
Address: Rue de Flandre 20
1000 Brussels, Belgium
Phone: 02 513 65 45

#60
Vismet
Cuisines: Seafood
Average price: Expensive
Area: Bruxelles, Centre-Ville
Address: Place Sainte-Catherine 23
1000 Brussels, Belgium
Phone: 02 218 85 45

#61
Le Wine Bar du Sablon des Marolles
Cuisines: Belgian
Average price: Expensive
Area: Bruxelles, Centre-Ville, Marolles
Address: Rue Haute 198
1000 Brussels, Belgium
Phone: 0496 82 01 05

#62
Sea Grill
Cuisines: Seafood
Average price: Exclusive
Area: Bruxelles, Centre-Ville
Address: Rue Fossé-aux-Loups 47
1000 Brussels, Belgium
Phone: 02 212 08 00

#63
Fanny Thai
Cuisines: Thai
Average price: Modest
Area: Bruxelles, Centre-Ville, Dansaert
Address: Rue Jules Van Praet 36
1000 Brussels, Belgium
Phone: 02 502 64 22

#64
Cô Nem
Cuisines: Vietnamese, Thai
Average price: Modest
Area: Bruxelles, Centre-Ville, Dansaert
Address: Rue Jules Van Preat 30
1000 Brussels, Belgium
Phone: 02 256 77 41

#65
Le Marmiton
Cuisines: French, Belgian
Average price: Expensive
Area: Bruxelles, Centre-Ville, Grand-Place
Address: Rue des Bouchers 43A
1000 Brussels, Belgium
Phone: 02 511 79 10

#66
La Bécasse
Cuisines: Bistro
Average price: Modest
Area: Bruxelles, Centre-Ville, Dansaert
Address: Rue de Tabora 11
1000 Brussels, Belgium
Phone: 02 511 00 06

#67
La Belle Equipe
Cuisines: Wine Bar, Pizza, Cafe
Average price: Modest
Area: Bruxelles, Centre-Ville, Dansaert
Address: Rue Antoine Dansaert 202
1000 Brussels, Belgium
Phone: 02 502 11 02

#68
La Tana
Cuisines: Italian, Beer Bar
Average price: Modest
Area: Bruxelles, Centre-Ville
Address: 10 rue de l'Enseignement
1000 Brussels, Belgium
Phone: 0489 73 19 16

#69
Les Caves du Sablon
Cuisines: French, Wine Bar
Average price: Expensive
Area: Bruxelles, Centre-Ville, Marolles
Address: Rue des Pigeons 9
1000 Brussels, Belgium
Phone: 02 513 12 20

#70
Green Mango
Cuisines: Juice Bar, Burgers
Average price: Modest
Area: Ixelles, Bruxelles, La Bascule, Louise
Address: Chaussée de Vleurgat 142
1000 Brussels, Belgium
Phone: 02 649 90 13

#71
Beijingya
Cuisines: Chinese
Average price: Modest
Area: Bruxelles, Centre-Ville
Address: Rue Melsens 6
1000 Brussels, Belgium
Phone: 02 514 36 88

#72
Friterie Tabora
Cuisines: Fast Food, Friterie
Average price: Inexpensive
Area: Bruxelles, Centre-Ville
Address: Rue de Tabora 2
1000 Brussels, Belgium
Phone: 02 514 92 14

#73
Au Vieux Saint Martin
Cuisines: Brasserie, Belgian
Average price: Expensive
Area: Bruxelles, Centre-Ville, Sablon
Address: Grand Sablon 38
1000 Brussels, Belgium
Phone: 02 512 64 76

#74
Bar Bik
Cuisines: European
Average price: Expensive
Area: Bruxelles, Centre-Ville
Address: Arduinkaai 3
1000 Brussels, Belgium
Phone: 02 219 75 00

#75
Kipkot
Cuisines: Belgian, Chicken Shop
Average price: Modest
Area: Ixelles, Matonge, Saint-Boniface
Address: Rue de la Paix 22
1050 Brussels, Belgium
Phone: 02 513 41 65

#76
Guinguette du Parc de Forest
Cuisines: Vegetarian, Vegan
Average price: Inexpensive
Area: Forest, Van Volxem - Van Haelen
Address: Parc de Forest
1190 Forest
Phone: 0475 50 67 41

#77
L'Intermezzo
Cuisines: Italian
Average price: Modest
Area: Bruxelles, Centre-Ville
Address: Rue des Princes 16
1000 Brussels, Belgium
Phone: 02 218 03 11

#78
Plaka
Cuisines: Greek
Average price: Inexpensive
Area: Bruxelles, Centre-Ville, Grand-Place
Address: Rue du Marché aux Fromages 6
1000 Brussels, Belgium
Phone: 02 511 21 27

#79
Les Halles Saint-Géry
Cuisines: Museums, Cafe
Average price: Modest
Area: Bruxelles, Centre-Ville, Dansaert
Address: Place Saint-Géry 23
1000 Brussels, Belgium
Phone: 02 502 44 24

#80
La Brocante
Cuisines: Belgian
Average price: Modest
Area: Bruxelles, Centre-Ville, Marolles
Address: Rue Blaes 170
1000 Brussels, Belgium
Phone: 02 512 13 43

#81
Le Coq
Cuisines: Cafe
Average price: Inexpensive
Area: Bruxelles, Centre-Ville, Dansaert
Address: Rue Auguste Orts 14
1000 Brussels, Belgium
Phone: 02 514 24 14

#82
Soul
Cuisines: European
Average price: Expensive
Area: Bruxelles, Centre-Ville, Marolles
Address: Rue de la Samaritaine 20
1000 Brussels, Belgium
Phone: 02 513 52 13

#83
Kokuban
Cuisines: Japanese
Average price: Modest
Area: Ixelles, Bruxelles, Etangs d'Ixelles,
La Bascule, Louise
Address: Rue Vilain XIIII 53-55
1000 Brussels, Belgium
Phone: 02 611 06 22

#84
Noordzee - Mer du Nord
Cuisines: Seafood, Fish & Chips
Average price: Modest
Area: Ixelles, Quartier Européen
Address: Rue du Luxembourg 62
1000 Brussels, Belgium
Phone: 02 280 05 00

#85
L'Océan
Cuisines: Seafood
Average price: Modest
Area: Bruxelles, Centre-Ville, Stalingrad
Address: Avenue de Stalingrad 94
1000 Brussels, Belgium
Phone: 02 513 30 38

#86
Het Goudblommeke in Papier
Cuisines: Cafe, Belgian
Average price: Modest
Area: Bruxelles, Centre-Ville, Stalingrad
Address: Rue des Alexiens 55
1000 Brussels, Belgium
Phone: 02 511 16 59

#87
Café Walvis
Cuisines: Cafe
Average price: Modest
Area: Bruxelles, Centre-Ville, Dansaert
Address: Rue Dansaert 209
1000 Brussels, Belgium
Phone: 02 219 95 32

#88
A L'Ombre de la Ville
Cuisines: Mediterranean, European
Average price: Modest
Area: Bruxelles, Centre-Ville, Quartier Royal
Address: Rue de la Reinette 7
1000 Brussels, Belgium
Phone: 0488 86 47 86

#89
Madame Chapeau
Cuisines: Bistro, Belgian
Average price: Modest
Area: Bruxelles, Centre-Ville, Stalingrad
Address: Rue du Marché Au Charbon 94
1000 Brussels, Belgium
Phone: 02 514 40 44

#90
La Marée
Cuisines: Seafood
Average price: Expensive
Area: Bruxelles, Centre-Ville
Address: Rue de Flandre 99
1000 Brussels, Belgium
Phone: 02 511 00 40

#91
Delish
Cuisines: Breakfast & Brunch,
Sandwiches, Coffee & Tea
Average price: Inexpensive
Area: Bruxelles, Centre-Ville
Address: Rue d'Arenberg 36
1000 Brussels, Belgium
Phone: 02 502 35 00

#92
9 et Voisins
Cuisines: Brasserie, Belgian
Average price: Modest
Area: Bruxelles, Centre-Ville, Dansaert
Address: Rue Van Artevelde 1
1000 Brussels, Belgium
Phone: 02 512 90 49

#93
Izaka-Ya
Cuisines: Japanese
Average price: Modest
Area: Ixelles, Bruxelles, Etangs d'Ixelles,
La Bascule, Louise
Address: Chaussée de Vleurgat 123
1000 Brussels, Belgium
Phone: 02 648 38 05

#94
Gramm
Cuisines: European, Asian Fusion
Average price: Expensive
Area: Bruxelles, Centre-Ville, Dansaert
Address: Rue de Flandre 86
1000 Brussels, Belgium
Phone: 02 324 99 66

#95
L'Estrille du Vieux Bruxelles
Cuisines: Belgian
Average price: Expensive
Area: Bruxelles, Centre-Ville, Marolles
Address: Rue de Rollebeek 7
1000 Brussels, Belgium
Phone: 02 512 58 57

#96
Toscana 21
Cuisines: Italian
Average price: Modest
Area: Bruxelles, Centre-Ville, Marolles
Address: Rue de Rollebeek 21
1000 Brussels, Belgium
Phone: 02 502 36 21

#97
Au Stekerlapatte
Cuisines: Belgian
Average price: Modest
Area: Bruxelles, Centre-Ville, Marolles
Address: Rue des Prêtres 4
1000 Brussels, Belgium
Phone: 02 512 86 81

#98
Café Georgette
Cuisines: Cafe, Brasserie
Average price: Expensive
Area: Bruxelles, Centre-Ville
Address: Rue de la Fourche 39
1000 Brussels, Belgium
Phone: 02 512 18 12

#99
CowFish
Cuisines: Burgers, Desserts, Seafood
Average price: Expensive
Area: Bruxelles, Centre-Ville, Sablon
Address: Rue du Pépin 39
1000 Brussels, Belgium
Phone: 02 503 04 03

#100
Tapas Locas
Cuisines: Tapas/Small Plates
Average price: Modest
Area: Bruxelles, Centre-Ville, Stalingrad
Address: Rue du Marché au Charbon 74
1000 Brussels, Belgium
Phone: 02 502 12 68

#101
Delicatessen
Cuisines: Salad, Delicatessen
Average price: Modest
Area: Bruxelles, Centre-Ville
Address: Rue Sainte-Catherine 17 - 19
1000 Brussels, Belgium
Phone: 02 324 78 79

#102
Toukoul
Cuisines: Ethiopian, Music Venue
Average price: Expensive
Area: Bruxelles, Centre-Ville
Address: Rue de Laeken 34
1000 Brussels, Belgium
Phone: 02 223 73 77

#103
Restaurant de l' Ogenblik
Cuisines: Belgian
Average price: Expensive
Area: Bruxelles, Centre-Ville
Address: Galerie des Princes 1
1000 Brussels, Belgium
Phone: 02 511 61 51

#104
Au Suisse
Cuisines: Sandwiches, Juice Bar,
Breakfast & Brunch
Average price: Modest
Area: Bruxelles, Centre-Ville, Dansaert
Address: Boulevard Anspach 73 75
1000 Brussels, Belgium
Phone: 02 512 95 89

#105
Cécila
Cuisines: Belgian, French
Average price: Exclusive
Area: Bruxelles, Centre-Ville, Stalingrad
Address: Hoedenmakersstraat 16
1000 Brussels, Belgium
Phone: 02 503 44 74

#106
Mr Falafel
Cuisines: Fast Food, Vegetarian
Average price: Inexpensive
Area: Bruxelles, Centre-Ville, Anneesens
Address: Boulevard Maurice Lemonnier 53
1000 Brussels, Belgium
Phone: 0493 34 64 12

#107
Pistolet-Original
Cuisines: Belgian
Average price: Modest
Area: Bruxelles, Centre-Ville, Marolles
Address: Rue Joseph Stevens 24
1000 Brussels, Belgium
Phone: 02 880 80 98

#108
A Casa Mia
Cuisines: Italian
Average price: Modest
Area: Bruxelles, Centre-Ville, Dansaert
Address: Rue de Flandre 50
1000 Brussels, Belgium
Phone: 02 513 45 77

#109
Cowfish Burgers
Cuisines: Burgers, Salad
Average price: Modest
Area: Bruxelles, Centre-Ville, Quartier Royal
Address: Rue de Pépin 48
1000 Brussels, Belgium
Phone: 02 514 28 00

#110
Maru
Cuisines: Korean
Average price: Expensive
Area: Ixelles
Address: Chaussee de Waterloo 510
1050 Brussels, Belgium
Phone: 02 346 11 11

#111
L'Express
Cuisines: Fast Food, Lebanese
Average price: Modest
Area: Bruxelles, Centre-Ville, Grand-Place
Address: Rue des Chapeliers 8
1000 Brussels, Belgium
Phone: 02 512 88 83

#112
Bar Recyclart
Cuisines: Bistro, Bar
Average price: Modest
Area: Bruxelles, Centre-Ville, Marolles
Address: Rue des Ursulines 25
1000 Brussels, Belgium
Phone: 02 502 57 34

#113
Turkish Grill
Cuisines: Turkish, Steakhouse
Average price: Modest
Area: Bruxelles, Centre-Ville, Martyrs
Address: 7 boulevard du Jardin Botanique
1000 Brussels, Belgium
Phone: 02 219 78 58

#114
Pipaillon-La Conserverie
Cuisines: Cafe, Belgian
Average price: Modest
Area: Bruxelles, Centre-Ville
Address: Quai au Bois à Brûler 11-13
1000 Brussels, Belgium
Phone: 02 201 22 08

#115
Manhattn's Burgers
Cuisines: Burgers
Average price: Modest
Area: Ixelles, Bruxelles, Louise
Address: Avenue Louise 164
1000 Brussels, Belgium
Phone: 02 649 85 95

#116
Les Vignes du Liban
Cuisines: Lebanese
Average price: Modest
Area: Bruxelles, Centre-Ville, Marolles
Address: 152 rue Haute
1000 Brussels, Belgium
Phone: 02 502 17 78

#117
Pin Pon
Cuisines: European, Breakfast & Brunch
Average price: Modest
Area: Bruxelles, Centre-Ville, Marolles
Address: Place du Jeu de Balle 62
1000 Brussels, Belgium
Phone: 02 540 89 99

#118
Le Corbeau
Cuisines: Bar, Brasserie
Average price: Modest
Area: Bruxelles, Centre-Ville, Martyrs
Address: Rue Saint-Michel 18
1000 Brussels, Belgium
Phone: 02 219 52 46

#119
The Music Village
Cuisines: Jazz & Blues, Venue & Event
Space, Brasserie
Average price: Modest
Area: Bruxelles, Centre-Ville, Grand-Place
Address: Rue des Pierres 50
1000 Brussels, Belgium
Phone: 02 513 13 45

#120
Bozar Brasserie
Cuisines: Brasserie, Belgian
Average price: Expensive
Area: Bruxelles, Centre-Ville, Quartier Royal
Address: Rue Baron Horta 3
1000 Brussels, Belgium
Phone: 02 503 00 00

#121
Al Piccolo Mondo
Cuisines: Italian, French, Belgian
Average price: Expensive
Area: Saint-Gilles
Address: Rue Jourdan 19
1060 Brussels, Belgium
Phone: 02 538 87 94

#122
Bistro du Canal
Cuisines: Bistro, Bar
Average price: Modest
Area: Bruxelles, Centre-Ville, Molenbeek-Saint-Jean, Dansaert
Address: Rue Antoine Dansaert 208
1000 Brussels, Belgium
Phone: 02 511 03 60

#123
Le Bugatti
Cuisines: Belgian
Average price: Expensive
Area: Ixelles, Bruxelles, La Bascule
Address: Rue Jacques Jordaens 4
1000 Brussels, Belgium
Phone: 02 646 14 17

#124
Pick Eat
Cuisines: Fast Food, Vegan, Breakfast & Brunch
Average price: Modest
Area: Ixelles, Matonge
Address: Rue de Dublin 19
1050 Brussels, Belgium
Phone: 0472 79 32 88

#125
Henri
Cuisines: European, Belgian
Average price: Expensive
Area: Bruxelles, Centre-Ville
Address: Rue de Flandre 113
1000 Brussels, Belgium
Phone: 02 218 00 08

#126
Moon Food
Cuisines: Vegetarian, Live/Raw Food, Vegan
Average price: Modest
Area: Bruxelles, Centre-Ville
Address: Rue des Colonies 58
1000 Brussels, Belgium
Phone: 02 303 43 32

#127
Le Roy d'Espagne
Cuisines: Belgian, Brasserie, Wine Bar
Average price: Expensive
Area: Bruxelles, Centre-Ville, Grand-Place
Address: Grand place 1
1000 Brussels, Belgium
Phone: 02 513 08 07

#128
Restobières
Cuisines: Belgian
Average price: Modest
Area: Bruxelles, Centre-Ville, Marolles
Address: Rue des Renards 9
1000 Brussels, Belgium
Phone: 02 511 55 83

#129
Le Chou de Bruxelles
Cuisines: Belgian
Average price: Expensive
Area: Ixelles, Chatelain
Address: Rue de Florence 26
1050 Brussels, Belgium
Phone: 02 537 69 95

#130
Le Crachin
Cuisines: Creperies
Average price: Modest
Area: Bruxelles, Centre-Ville, Dansaert
Address: Rue de Flandre 12
1000 Brussels, Belgium
Phone: 02 502 13 00

#131
La Cantina
Cuisines: Brazilian
Average price: Modest
Area: Bruxelles, Centre-Ville, Stalingrad
Address: Rue du Jardin des Olives 13-15
1000 Brussels, Belgium
Phone: 02 513 42 76

#132
Machu Picchu El Huarique Peruvien
Cuisines: Peruvian
Average price: Modest
Area: Saint-Gilles, Porte de Hal
Address: Rue de Mérode 7
1060 Brussels, Belgium
Phone: 0484 27 99 43

#133
The Restaurant By Pierre Balthazar
Cuisines: Lounge, Cafe
Average price: Exclusive
Area: Bruxelles, Sablon
Address: Bd de Waterloo 38
1000 Brussels, Belgium
Phone: 02 504 13 33

#134
Skievelat
Cuisines: Brasserie, Belgian
Average price: Modest
Area: Bruxelles, Centre-Ville, Marolles
Address: Rue Joseph Stevens 16-18
1000 Brussels, Belgium
Phone: 02 502 25 12

#135
Mirante Pizzeria
Cuisines: Pizza, Italian
Average price: Modest
Area: Bruxelles, Centre-Ville, Dansaert
Address: Plattesteen 13
1000 Brussels, Belgium
Phone: 02 511 15 80

#136
Asia Grill
Cuisines: Asian Fusion
Average price: Inexpensive
Area: Bruxelles, Centre-Ville, Stalingrad
Address: Rue du Marche au Charbon 98
1000 Brussels, Belgium
Phone: 02 512 52 08

#137
Ty Penty
Cuisines: Food Truck, Creperies
Average price: Inexpensive
Area: Saint-Gilles
Address: Marché de la Place Van Meenen
1060 Brussels, Belgium
Phone: 0478 87 29 63

#138
King Kong
Cuisines: Peruvian, Fast Food
Average price: Modest
Area: Saint-Gilles, Ma Campagne, Berckmans
- Hotel des Monnaies
Address: Chaussée de Charleroi 227
1060 Brussels, Belgium
Phone: 02 537 01 96

#139
Genco
Cuisines: Italian
Average price: Expensive
Area: Bruxelles, Centre-Ville, Marolles
Address: Rue Joseph Stevens 28
1000 Brussels, Belgium
Phone: 02 511 34 44

#140
La Grainerie
Cuisines: Cafe, Delicatessen, Vegan
Average price: Inexpensive
Area: Ixelles
Address: Rue de Tenbosch 112
1050 Brussels, Belgium
Phone: 02 217 98 27

#141
Yaki
Cuisines: Thai, Vietnamese
Average price: Modest
Area: Bruxelles, Centre-Ville, Dansaert
Address: Rue des Poissonniers 6
1000 Brussels, Belgium
Phone: 02 503 28 58

#142
Black Sheep
Cuisines: GastroPub
Average price: Modest
Area: Ixelles, Flagey, Etangs d'Ixelles
Address: Chausee De Boondael 8
1050 Brussels, Belgium
Phone: 02 644 38 03

#143
Fritland
Cuisines: Fast Food, Friterie, Belgian
Average price: Inexpensive
Area: Bruxelles, Centre-Ville, Dansaert
Address: Rue Henri Maus 49
1000 Brussels, Belgium
Phone: 02 514 06 27

#144
Royal Brasserie Brussels
Cuisines: Belgian
Average price: Exclusive
Area: Bruxelles, Centre-Ville
Address: Vlaamsesteenweg 103
1000 Brussels, Belgium
Phone: 02 217 85 00

#145
Le Bistro
Cuisines: Belgian, European, Cafe
Average price: Modest
Area: Bruxelles, Marolles
Address: Boulevard de Waterloo 138
1000 Brussels, Belgium
Phone: 02 539 44 54

#146
Les Canailles du Châtelain
Cuisines: French
Average price: Modest
Area: Ixelles, Chatelain
Address: 38 rue du Bailli
1000 Brussels, Belgium
Phone: 02 647 06 16

#147
Les Larmes du Tigre
Cuisines: Asian Fusion, Thai
Average price: Expensive
Area: Bruxelles, Centre-Ville, Marolles
Address: Rue de Wynants 21
1000 Brussels, Belgium
Phone: 02 512 18 77

#148
Chez Willy
Cuisines: Belgian, French, European
Average price: Expensive
Area: Bruxelles, Centre-Ville, Grand-Place
Address: 14 rue de la Fourche
1000 Brussels, Belgium
Phone: 0471 65 08 27

#149
Chicago Café
Cuisines: Breakfast & Brunch, Venue & Event
Space, Cafe
Average price: Modest
Area: Bruxelles, Centre-Ville
Address: Rue de Flandre 45
1000 Brussels, Belgium
Phone: 02 502 18 41

#150
La Belle Maraichère
Cuisines: Seafood
Average price: Expensive
Area: Bruxelles, Centre-Ville
Address: Place Sainte-Catherine 11
1000 Brussels, Belgium
Phone: 02 512 97 59

#151
La Marie Joseph
Cuisines: Fish & Chips, Seafood
Average price: Expensive
Area: Bruxelles, Centre-Ville
Address: Quai au Bois à Brûler 47-49
1000 Brussels, Belgium
Phone: 02 218 05 96

#152
Madagasikara
Cuisines: African, Caribbean
Average price: Expensive
Area: Bruxelles, Centre-Ville, Dansaert
Address: Rue de Flandre 10
1000 Brussels, Belgium
Phone: 0473 44 40 74

#153
À La Mort Subite
Cuisines: Brasserie, Belgian
Average price: Modest
Area: Bruxelles, Centre-Ville
Address: Rue Montagne aux Herbes
Potagères 7
1000 Brussels, Belgium
Phone: 02 513 13 18

#154
The Old Oak
Cuisines: Irish, Pub
Average price: Modest
Area: Bruxelles, Quartier Européen
Address: Rue Franklin 26
1000 Brussels, Belgium
Phone: 0489 73 76 57

#155
Umamido
Cuisines: Japanese
Average price: Modest
Area: Bruxelles, Centre-Ville
Address: Place Sainte-Catherine 1
1000 Brussels, Belgium
Phone: 02 511 62 21

#156
Chez WaWa
Cuisines: Mexican
Average price: Modest
Area: Ixelles, Chatelain
Address: Rue Américaine 91
1050 Brussels, Belgium
Phone: 02 534 63 30

#157
L'Arrière Pays
Cuisines: Brasserie
Average price: Modest
Area: Bruxelles, Centre-Ville, Sablon
Address: Rue des Minimes 60
1000 Brussels, Belgium
Phone: 02 514 77 07

#158
La Manufacture
Cuisines: European
Average price: Expensive
Area: Bruxelles, Centre-Ville, Dansaert
Address: Rue Notre-Dame du Sommeil 12
1000 Brussels, Belgium
Phone: 02 502 25 25

#159
Damejeanne Café
Cuisines: Cafe, Bar, Italian
Average price: Inexpensive
Area: Bruxelles, Centre-Ville
Address: Boulevard d'Ypres 33
1000 Brussels, Belgium
Phone: 0488 69 96 19

#160
Green kitchen
Cuisines: Salad, Sandwiches
Average price: Modest
Area: Bruxelles, Centre-Ville, Quartier Royal
Address: Place Royale 9
1000 Brussels, Belgium
Phone: 02 545 08 09

#161
Paradiso
Cuisines: Italian
Average price: Modest
Area: Bruxelles, Centre-Ville, Quartier Royal
Address: Rue Duquesnoy 34
1000 Brussels, Belgium
Phone: 02 512 52 32

#162
Café Novo
Cuisines: European, Cafe
Average price: Modest
Area: Bruxelles, Centre-Ville, Stalingrad
Address: Place de la Vieille Halle aux Blés 37
1000 Brussels, Belgium
Phone: 02 503 09 05

#163
The Deli
Cuisines: American
Average price: Inexpensive
Area: Bruxelles, Centre-Ville
Address: Rue d'Arenberg 32
1000 Brussels, Belgium
Phone: 02 502 35 00

#164
La Piola Libri
Cuisines: Italian
Average price: Modest
Area: Bruxelles, Quartier Européen
Address: Rue Franklin 66-68
1000 Brussels, Belgium
Phone: 02 736 93 91

#165
Da-Kao II
Cuisines: Vietnamese
Average price: Modest
Area: Bruxelles, Centre-Ville, Dansaert
Address: Rue Van Artevelde 19
1000 Brussels, Belgium
Phone: 02 512 67 16

#166
Parfum d'Asie
Cuisines: Sushi Bar
Average price: Modest
Area: Bruxelles, Centre-Ville
Address: Rue Royale 115
1000 Brussels, Belgium
Phone: 0479 76 83 42

#167
Natural caffè Mont des Arts
Cuisines: Coffee & Tea, Sandwiches, Salad
Average price: Modest
Area: Bruxelles, Centre-Ville, Quartier Royal
Address: Rue Mont des Arts 20
1000 Brussels, Belgium
Phone: 02 502 20 54

#168
Dilmon la Table D'Orient
Cuisines: Mediterranean, Lebanese
Average price: Modest
Area: Bruxelles, Saint-Josse-Ten-Noode
Address: Chaussée de Louvain 217
1210 Brussels, Belgium
Phone: 02 732 61 63

#169
Den Talurelekker
Cuisines: Belgian, European
Average price: Modest
Area: Bruxelles, Centre-Ville
Address: Rue de l'Enseignement 25
1000 Brussels, Belgium
Phone: 02 219 30 25

#170
Dam Sum
Cuisines: Dim Sum
Average price: Modest
Area: Ixelles, Chatelain
Address: Parvis de la Trinite 11
1050 Brussels, Belgium
Phone: 02 538 08 10

#171
Belga Queen
Cuisines: Belgian, Lounge
Average price: Exclusive
Area: Bruxelles, Centre-Ville
Address: Rue du Fossé aux Loups 32
1000 Brussels, Belgium
Phone: 02 217 21 87

#172
Aux Gaufres de Bruxelles
Cuisines: French, Tea Room, Sandwiches
Average price: Inexpensive
Area: Bruxelles, Centre-Ville, Grand-Place
Address: Rue marché aux herbes 113
1000 Brussels, Belgium
Phone: 02 514 01 71

#173
Per Bacco
Cuisines: Pizza, Italian
Average price: Modest
Area: Bruxelles, Centre-Ville
Address: Rue de l'Enseignement 31
1000 Brussels, Belgium
Phone: 02 217 00 17

#174
Boom
Cuisines: Cafe
Average price: Inexpensive
Area: Bruxelles, Centre-Ville, Dansaert
Address: Rue Pletinckx 7
1000 Brussels, Belgium
Phone: 02 736 51 10

#175
Kom Bij Mâ
Cuisines: Belgian, Brasserie
Average price: Expensive
Area: Bruxelles, Centre-Ville
Address: Place Sainte Catherine 3
1000 Brussels, Belgium
Phone: 02 502 35 73

#176
La Meilleure Jeunesse
Cuisines: French
Average price: Expensive
Area: Ixelles, Bruxelles, Louise
Address: Rue de l'Aurore 58
1000 Brussels, Belgium
Phone: 02 640 23 94

#177
Le Perroquet
Cuisines: Brasserie, Fast Food
Average price: Modest
Area: Bruxelles, Centre-Ville, Sablon
Address: Rue Watteeu 31
1000 Brussels, Belgium
Phone: 02 512 99 22

#178
Chez Patrick
Cuisines: European, Belgian
Average price: Modest
Area: Bruxelles, Centre-Ville, Grand-Place
Address: Rue des Chapeliers 6
1000 Brussels, Belgium
Phone: 02 511 98 15

#179
Bossa Nova
Cuisines: Buffet, Brazilian
Average price: Modest
Area: Bruxelles, Centre-Ville, Marolles
Address: Rue Haute 381
1000 Brussels, Belgium
Phone: 0472 80 25 73

#180
Chez Andriana
Cuisines: Greek, Grocery,
Convenience Store
Average price: Inexpensive
Area: Bruxelles, Centre-Ville, Anneessens
Address: Rue de la Poudrière 46
1000 Brussels, Belgium
Phone: 02 513 22 39

#181
LOFT
Cuisines: Steakhouse, Burgers, Cocktail Bar
Average price: Modest
Area: Bruxelles, Centre-Ville, Quartier Royal
Address: Rue de Namur 51
1000 Brussels, Belgium
Phone: 02 511 52 11

#182
Vini Divini Aperitivi
Cuisines: Italian
Average price: Expensive
Area: Ixelles, Matonge
Address: Rue du Berger 24
1050 Brussels, Belgium
Phone: 02 502 03 80

#183
Chaochow City
Cuisines: Asian Fusion
Average price: Inexpensive
Area: Bruxelles, Centre-Ville, Dansaert
Address: Bd Anspach 89
1000 Brussels, Belgium
Phone: 02 512 82 83

#184
Poissonnerie ABC
Cuisines: Seafood Market, Tapas Bar
Average price: Modest
Area: Bruxelles, Centre-Ville, Dansaert
Address: Rue Sainte-Catherine 46
1000 Brussels, Belgium
Phone: 02 512 75 47

#185
Bistrot du Luxembourg
Cuisines: Bistro, Brasserie
Average price: Modest
Area: Ixelles, Quartier Européen
Address: Rue du Luxembourg 43
1000 Brussels, Belgium
Phone: 02 503 61 70

#186
Les Petits Oignons
Cuisines: French
Average price: Expensive
Area: Bruxelles, Centre-Ville, Sablon
Address: Rue de la Régence 25
1000 Brussels, Belgium
Phone: 02 511 76 15

#187
Chez Mauricette
Cuisines: Salad, Fast Food, Soup
Average price: Modest
Area: Bruxelles, Quartier Européen
Address: Rue Belliard 170-174
1000 Brussels, Belgium
Phone: 02 230 40 46

#188
Amadeo - Amadeus
Cuisines: Barbeque, American
Average price: Modest
Area: Bruxelles, Centre-Ville, Dansaert
Address: Rue Sainte Catherine 26
1000 Brussels, Belgium
Phone: 0495 16 77 53

#189
Chaff
Cuisines: Cafe, European, Belgian
Average price: Modest
Area: Bruxelles, Centre-Ville, Marolles
Address: Place du Jeu de Balle 21
1000 Brussels, Belgium
Phone: 02 502 58 48

#190
Mémé Café
Cuisines: Mediterranean
Average price: Inexpensive
Area: Bruxelles, Centre-Ville, Dansaert
Address: Rue des Riches Claires 17
1000 Brussels, Belgium
Phone: 0486 55 57 25

#191
Le Temps d'une Pose
Cuisines: French
Average price: Modest
Area: Bruxelles, Centre-Ville
Address: rue de Laeken, 116
1000 Brussels, Belgium
Phone: 02 229 41 29

#192
Maison du Cygne
Cuisines: Belgian
Average price: Exclusive
Area: Bruxelles, Centre-Ville, Grand-Place
Address: Grand-Place 9
1000 Brussels, Belgium
Phone: 02 511 82 44

#193
Meet Meat
Cuisines: Steakhouse, Argentine
Average price: Expensive
Area: Bruxelles, Quartier Européen
Address: Rue Stevin 124
1000 Brussels, Belgium
Phone: 02 231 07 42

#194
La Roue d'Or
Cuisines: Brasserie, Belgian, French
Average price: Expensive
Area: Bruxelles, Centre-Ville, Grand-Place
Address: Rue des Chapeliers 26
1000 Brussels, Belgium
Phone: 02 514 25 54

#195
Corica
Cuisines: Cafe, Coffee Roasteries
Average price: Modest
Area: Bruxelles, Centre-Ville, Dansaert
Address: Rue du Marché aux Poulets 49
1000 Brussels, Belgium
Phone: 02 511 88 52

#196
Hellas
Cuisines: Kebab
Average price: Inexpensive
Area: Bruxelles, Centre-Ville, Grand-Place
Address: Rue marche aux fromages, 4
1000 Brussels, Belgium
Phone: 02 512 01 20

#197
Fait Maison
Cuisines: Cafe
Average price: Inexpensive
Area: Ixelles, Bruxelles, La Bascule
Address: Chaussée de Vleurgat 158
1000 Brussels, Belgium
Phone: 02 648 19 31

#198
In't Spinnekopke
Cuisines: Belgian
Average price: Expensive
Area: Bruxelles, Centre-Ville, Dansaert
Address: Place du Jardin aux Fleurs 1
1000 Brussels, Belgium
Phone: 02 511 86 95

#199
Le Bier Circus
Cuisines: Cafe
Average price: Modest
Area: Bruxelles, Centre-Ville
Address: Rue de l'Enseignement 57
1000 Brussels, Belgium
Phone: 02 218 00 34

#200
Spago
Cuisines: Italian
Average price: Modest
Area: Bruxelles, Centre-Ville, Dansaert
Address: Rue du Pont de la Carpe 13
1000 Brussels, Belgium
Phone: 02 512 25 30

#201
La Taverne du Passage
Cuisines: French, Belgian
Average price: Expensive
Area: Bruxelles, Centre-Ville, Grand-Place
Address: Galerie de la Reine 30
1000 Brussels, Belgium
Phone: 02 512 37 31

#202
Lulu Home Interior & Café
Cuisines: Furniture Store, Home Decor, Cafe
Average price: Modest
Area: Ixelles, Ma Campagne
Address: Rue du Page 101
1050 Brussels, Belgium
Phone: 02 537 25 03

#203
Le Petit Coin Royal
Cuisines: Sandwiches
Average price: Inexpensive
Area: Bruxelles, Centre-Ville
Address: Rue de l'association 4
1000 Brussels, Belgium
Phone: 02 223 71 00

#204
Mangetsu
Cuisines: Cafe
Average price: Expensive
Area: Bruxelles, Centre-Ville, Grand-Place
Address: Rue de la Fourche 13
1000 Brussels, Belgium
Phone: 02 511 83 67

#205
Winery Schuman
Cuisines: Wine Bar, Beer, Wine & Spirits,
Tapas/Small Plates
Average price: Modest
Area: Bruxelles, Quartier Européen
Address: Rue Juste Lipse 17
1000 Brussels, Belgium
Phone: 02 231 69 89

#206
Mamma Mia Restaurant
Cuisines: Mediterranean, Pizza, Italian
Average price: Modest
Area: Bruxelles, Centre-Ville, Dansaert
Address: Rue Antoine Dansaert 158
1000 Brussels, Belgium
Phone: 02 513 44 40

#207
Bij den Boer
Cuisines: Seafood, Belgian
Average price: Expensive
Area: Bruxelles, Centre-Ville
Address: Quai aux briques 60
1000 Brussels, Belgium
Phone: 02 512 61 22

#208
Arcadi
Cuisines: French, Bistro, Cafe
Average price: Modest
Area: Bruxelles, Centre-Ville
Address: Rue d'Arenbean 1b
1000 Brussels, Belgium
Phone: 02 511 33 43

#209
Yeti
Cuisines: Indian, American
Average price: Inexpensive
Area: Bruxelles, Centre-Ville, Stalingrad
Address: Rue de Bon Secours 4
1000 Brussels, Belgium
Phone: 02 502 24 26

#210
La Rose Blanche
Cuisines: Belgian
Average price: Modest
Area: Bruxelles, Centre-Ville, Grand-Place
Address: Grand place 11
1000 Brussels, Belgium
Phone: 02 513 64 79

#211
Le NewDaric
Cuisines: Cafe
Average price: Modest
Area: Bruxelles, Centre-Ville
Address: Place de la Liberté 8
1000 Brussels, Belgium
Phone: 02 218 06 43

#212
Puerta Nueva
Cuisines: Italian, Pizza, Spanish
Average price: Modest
Area: Bruxelles, Centre-Ville
Address: Quai au Bois A Brûler 3a -3b
1000 Brussels, Belgium
Phone: 02 840 67 98

#213
De la Vigne à l'Assiette
Cuisines: French
Average price: Exclusive
Area: Ixelles, Bruxelles
Address: Rue de la Longue Haie 51
1000 Brussels, Belgium
Phone: 02 647 68 03

#214
Le Dauphin
Cuisines: Cafe
Average price: Modest
Area: Bruxelles, Quartier Européen
Address: Rue du Luxembourg 12
1000 Brussels, Belgium
Phone: 02 502 59 21

#215
Waffle Factory
Cuisines: Waffles
Average price: Inexpensive
Area: Bruxelles, Centre-Ville, Grand-Place
Address: Rue du Lombard 30
1000 Brussels, Belgium
Phone: 02 502 31 47

#216
Rock Salt Chilli Peppers
Cuisines: Asian Fusion
Average price: Expensive
Area: Bruxelles, Centre-Ville
Address: Rue Des Cultes 34-36
1000 Brussels, Belgium
Phone: 0498 36 92 29

#217
La Focaccia Pazza
Cuisines: Breakfast & Brunch, Sandwiches
Average price: Inexpensive
Area: Bruxelles, Centre-Ville, Martyrs
Address: Rue du Marais 100
1000 Brussels, Belgium
Phone: 02 219 36 30

#218
'T Kelderke
Cuisines: Belgian
Average price: Expensive
Area: Bruxelles, Centre-Ville, Grand-Place
Address: Grand place 15
1000 Brussels, Belgium
Phone: 02 513 73 44

#219
L'Orchidée Rose
Cuisines: Vietnamese, Thai
Average price: Modest
Area: Bruxelles, Centre-Ville, Dansaert
Address: 16 rue Van Artevelde
1000 Brussels, Belgium
Phone: 0475 79 67 86

#220
Or Espresso Bar
Cuisines: Cafe
Average price: Inexpensive
Area: Bruxelles, Centre-Ville, Dansaert
Address: Rue Auguste Orts 9
1000 Brussels, Belgium
Phone: 02 511 74 00

#221
Al Barmaki
Cuisines: Lebanese
Average price: Expensive
Area: Bruxelles, Centre-Ville, Grand-Place
Address: Rue des Eperonniers 67
1000 Brussels, Belgium
Phone: 02 513 08 34

#222
Ricotta & Parmesan
Cuisines: Italian, Venue & Event Space
Average price: Modest
Area: Bruxelles, Centre-Ville
Address: Rue de l'Ecuyer 31
1000 Brussels, Belgium
Phone: 02 502 80 82

#223
Caspian
Cuisines: Persian/Iranian
Average price: Modest
Area: Bruxelles, Centre-Ville, Grand-Place
Address: Rue de la Violette 26
1000 Brussels, Belgium
Phone: 02 513 15 11

#224
L'Atelier de Jean
Cuisines: French
Average price: Modest
Area: Bruxelles, Centre-Ville, Sablon
Address: Rue du Grand Cerf 20
1000 Brussels, Belgium
Phone: 02 513 05 00

#225
Exki
Cuisines: Sandwiches, Salad
Average price: Modest
Area: Bruxelles, Centre-Ville, Grand-Place
Address: Rue du Marché aux Herbes 93
1000 Brussels, Belgium
Phone: 02 502 82 48

#226
Mont Liban
Cuisines: Lebanese
Average price: Modest
Area: Ixelles, Chatelain
Address: Rue de Livourne 30
1000 Brussels, Belgium
Phone: 02 537 71 31

#227
Michael Collins
Cuisines: Cafe, Irish Pub, Breakfast & Brunch
Average price: Modest
Area: Ixelles, Bruxelles, Louise
Address: Rue du Bailli 1
1000 Brussels, Belgium
Phone: 02 644 61 21

#228
Taverne Greenwich
Cuisines: Belgian
Average price: Modest
Area: Bruxelles, Centre-Ville, Dansaert
Address: Rue des Chartreux 7
1000 Brussels, Belgium
Phone: 02 540 88 78

#229
Coming Soon
Cuisines: Bistro, Brasserie
Average price: Inexpensive
Area: Bruxelles, Centre-Ville, Stalingrad
Address: Place de la Vieille Halle aux Blés 34
1000 Brussels, Belgium
Phone: 02 325 78 10

#230
Chez Soje
Cuisines: Belgian
Average price: Expensive
Area: Jette, Basilique
Address: 85 avenue de Jette
1090 Brussels, Belgium
Phone: 02 427 55 52

#231
Le Roi des Belges
Cuisines: Bistro
Average price: Modest
Area: Bruxelles, Centre-Ville, Dansaert
Address: Rue Jules van Praet 35
1000 Brussels, Belgium
Phone: 02 513 51 16

#232
La Villa In The Sky
Cuisines: Cafe
Average price: Exclusive
Area: Ixelles, Bruxelles, Louise
Address: Avenue Louise 480
1050 Brussels, Belgium
Phone: 0496 80 89 89

#233
Le Petit Palais
Cuisines: Belgian
Average price: Expensive
Area: Bruxelles, Centre-Ville, Quartier Royal
Address: Rue du Baudet 5
1000 Brussels, Belgium
Phone: 02 512 10 12

#234
Via Balbi
Cuisines: Italian
Average price: Modest
Area: Bruxelles, Porte De Namur, Centre-
Ville, Quartier Royal
Address: Rue de Namur 80
1000 Brussels, Belgium
Phone: 0485 52 15 95

#235
Place de Londres Café
Cuisines: Lounge, Bistro, Belgian
Average price: Modest
Area: Ixelles, Matonge
Address: Place de Londres 13
1050 Brussels, Belgium
Phone: 02 502 21 37

#236
Panos
Cuisines: Sandwiches
Average price: Inexpensive
Area: Bruxelles, Centre-Ville, Grand-Place
Address: Grasmarkt 85
1000 Brussels, Belgium
Phone: 02 513 14 43

#237
Chez Léon
Cuisines: Belgian, Seafood
Average price: Expensive
Area: Bruxelles, Centre-Ville
Address: Rue des Bouchers 18
1000 Brussels, Belgium
Phone: 02 511 14 15

#238
Mr Patate
Cuisines: Fast Food
Average price: Inexpensive
Area: Bruxelles, Centre-Ville
Address: Emile Jaquemain 44
1000 Brussels, Belgium
Phone: 0485 87 23 27

#239
La Bellone Café
Cuisines: French, Cafe, Tapas Bar
Average price: Modest
Area: Bruxelles, Centre-Ville
Address: Rue de Flandre 46
1000 Brussels, Belgium
Phone: 0472 35 10 91

#240
Enjoy Brussels
Cuisines: French
Average price: Expensive
Area: Bruxelles, Sablon
Address: Boulevard de Waterloo 22
1000 Brussels, Belgium
Phone: 02 641 57 90

#241
Yummy
Cuisines: Soup, Sandwiches, Vegan
Average price: Modest
Area: Bruxelles, Quartier Européen
Address: Rue de la Loi 19
1000 Brussels, Belgium
Phone: 02 280 25 08

#242
Easy Tempo
Cuisines: Italian
Average price: Modest
Area: Bruxelles, Centre-Ville, Marolles
Address: Rue Haute 146
1000 Brussels, Belgium
Phone: 02 513 54 40

#243
EL Fontan
Cuisines: Spanish, Tapas Bar
Average price: Inexpensive
Area: Bruxelles, Centre-Ville, Marolles
Address: Rue Haute 179
1000 Brussels, Belgium
Phone: 02 502 35 59

#244
Il Passa Tempo
Cuisines: Italian
Average price: Expensive
Area: Bruxelles, Centre-Ville, Quartier Royal
Address: Rue Namur 32
1000 Brussels, Belgium
Phone: 02 511 37 03

#245
Cafe Bebo
Cuisines: Cafe, Bistro, Bar
Average price: Modest
Area: Bruxelles, Centre-Ville, Stalingrad
Address: Avenue de Stalingrad 2
1000 Brussels, Belgium
Phone: 02 514 71 11

#246
Kick Tap'Ass
Cuisines: Tapas Bar
Average price: Modest
Area: Bruxelles, Centre-Ville
Address: Rue de Laeken 54
1000 Brussels, Belgium
Phone: 0498 48 17 31

#247
Maxi-Bagi
Cuisines: Sandwiches
Average price: Inexpensive
Area: Bruxelles, Centre-Ville, Martyrs
Address: Passage Du Nord
1000 Brussels, Belgium
Phone: 02 217 71 00

#248
Pepete & Ronron
Cuisines: Wine Bar, Tapas, Delicatessen
Average price: Modest
Area: Bruxelles, Centre-Ville, Dansaert
Address: Rue Léon Lepage 53
1000 Brussels, Belgium
Phone: 02 513 33 49

#249
Ellis Gourmet Burger
Cuisines: Burgers, American
Average price: Modest
Area: Bruxelles, Centre-Ville
Address: Place sainte-Catherine 4
1000 Brussels, Belgium
Phone: 02 514 23 14

#250
Davi
Cuisines: Thai
Average price: Modest
Area: Bruxelles, Centre-Ville, Dansaert
Address: Rue Jules Van Praet 20- 22
1000 Brussels, Belgium
Phone: 02 511 18 21

#251
The Sister Brussels Cafe
Cuisines: Beer Bar, Cafe
Average price: Modest
Area: Bruxelles, Centre-Ville, Grand-Place
Address: Rue Chair et Pain 3
1000 Brussels, Belgium
Phone: 02 513 22 26

#252
Mykonos
Cuisines: Greek, Fast Food
Average price: Inexpensive
Area: Bruxelles, Centre-Ville, Grand-Place
Address: Rue du Marché aux Fromages 8
1000 Brussels, Belgium
Phone: 02 513 73 54

#253
Bunny Snack
Cuisines: Cafeteria
Average price: Modest
Area: Bruxelles, Centre-Ville, Martyrs
Address: Rue Neuve 123
1000 Brussels, Belgium
Phone: 02 218 38 00

#254
Le Café Gudule
Cuisines: Burgers
Average price: Modest
Area: Bruxelles, Centre-Ville
Address: Rue du Gentilhomme 11
1000 Brussels, Belgium
Phone: 02 503 10 15

#255
Le Nil
Cuisines: Middle Eastern, Belgian
Average price: Modest
Area: Bruxelles, Centre-Ville, Anneesens
Address: Boulevard Maurice Lemonnier 165
1000 Brussels, Belgium
Phone: 02 513 13 51

#256
La Baie d'Ha-long
Cuisines: Vietnamese
Average price: Modest
Area: Bruxelles, Quartier Européen
Address: Rue Stévin 180
1000 Brussels, Belgium
Phone: 02 734 54 38

#257
Thai Coffee
Cuisines: Thai
Average price: Modest
Area: Bruxelles, Centre-Ville
Address: Rue du Congrès 50
1000 Brussels, Belgium
Phone: 02 212 07 00

#258
Bruno
Cuisines: Italian
Average price: Modest
Area: Ixelles, Bruxelles, La Bascule
Address: Chaussée de Vleurgat 186
1000 Brussels, Belgium
Phone: 02 648 26 64

#259
Cŏcīna
Cuisines: Italian, Delicatessen
Average price: Expensive
Area: Ixelles
Address: Rue Washington 149
1050 Brussels, Belgium
Phone: 02 850 59 90

#260
La Canne à Sucre
Cuisines: Cajun/Creole, Lounge
Average price: Exclusive
Area: Bruxelles, Centre-Ville, Marolles
Address: Rue des Pigeons 12
1000 Brussels, Belgium
Phone: 02 513 03 72

#261
Ciabatta Mania
Cuisines: Sandwiches, Juice Bar
Average price: Inexpensive
Area: Bruxelles, Centre-Ville, Quartier Royal
Address: Coudenberg 70
1000 Brussels, Belgium
Phone: 02 502 06 03

#262
Fornostar
Cuisines: Pizza
Average price: Expensive
Area: Bruxelles, Centre-Ville
Address: 65 quai au Bois à Brûler
1000 Brussels, Belgium
Phone: 02 201 30 22

#263
Le Temps des Tartines
Cuisines: Cafe, Bakery, Coffee & Tea
Average price: Modest
Area: Bruxelles, Centre-Ville, Stalingrad
Address: Rue du Midi 71
1000 Brussels, Belgium
Phone: 02 503 29 00

#264
Sara's Id
Cuisines: Cafe
Average price: Modest
Area: Bruxelles, Centre-Ville
Address: Rue du Marché aux Poulets 2
1000 Brussels, Belgium
Phone: 02 218 01 01

#265
K-NAL
Cuisines: Dance Club, European
Average price: Modest
Area: Bruxelles, Quartier Maritime
Address: Ave du Port 1
1000 Brussels, Belgium
Phone: 02 427 26 91

#266
Comocomo
Cuisines: Spanish, Basque, Tapas Bar
Average price: Modest
Area: Bruxelles, Centre-Ville, Dansaert
Address: Antoine Dansaert 19
1000 Brussels, Belgium
Phone: 02 503 03 30

#267
Bla Bla & Gallery
Cuisines: Mediterranean,
Breakfast & Brunch, Belgian
Average price: Modest
Area: Bruxelles, Centre-Ville, Marolles
Address: Rue des Capucins 51-55
1000 Brussels, Belgium
Phone: 02 503 59 18

#268
Friture Pitta de la Chapelle
Cuisines: Belgian
Average price: Inexpensive
Area: Bruxelles, Centre-Ville, Marolles
Address: Place de la Chapelle 15
1000 Brussels, Belgium
Phone: 02 514 06 36

#269
Les Chapeliers
Cuisines: Belgian
Average price: Expensive
Area: Bruxelles, Centre-Ville, Grand-Place
Address: Rue des Chapeliers 1
1000 Brussels, Belgium
Phone: 02 513 64 79

#270
Saco
Cuisines: Pizza
Average price: Expensive
Area: Bruxelles, Centre-Ville
Address: Rue de la Croix de Fer 39
1000 Brussels, Belgium
Phone: 02 511 02 07

#271
Signora Ava
Cuisines: Italian
Average price: Modest
Area: Bruxelles, Centre-Ville, Dansaert
Address: Rue de Flandre 92
1000 Brussels, Belgium
Phone: 04 66335925

#272
Notos
Cuisines: Greek
Average price: Exclusive
Area: Ixelles, Bruxelles, Chatelain
Address: Rue de Livourne 154
1000 Brussels, Belgium
Phone: 02 513 29 59

#273
L'Atlantide
Cuisines: Greek
Average price: Expensive
Area: Bruxelles, Quartier Européen
Address: Rue Franklin 73
1000 Brussels, Belgium
Phone: 02 736 20 02

#274
Le Santouri
Cuisines: Greek
Average price: Expensive
Area: Bruxelles, Centre-Ville, Marolles
Address: Rue de Rollebeek 10
1000 Brussels, Belgium
Phone: 02 512 65 00

#275
Théâtre Royal de Toone
Cuisines: Cafe
Average price: Inexpensive
Area: Bruxelles, Centre-Ville, Grand-Place
Address: 66 Rue Marché aux Herbes
1000 Brussels, Belgium
Phone: 02 513 54 86

#276
Mi Tango
Cuisines: Argentine
Average price: Expensive
Area: Bruxelles
Address: Rue de Spa 31
1000 Brussels, Belgium
Phone: 02 230 99 95

#277
Le Titanic
Cuisines: Brasserie, Belgian, French
Average price: Expensive
Area: Bruxelles, Centre-Ville
Address: Rue du Congrès 31
1000 Brussels, Belgium
Phone: 02 219 99 10

#278
Big Mama
Cuisines: French, Belgian
Average price: Modest
Area: Bruxelles, Centre-Ville, Stalingrad
Address: Place de la Vieille Halle aux Blés 41
1000 Brussels, Belgium
Phone: 02 513 36 59

#279
El Vasco
Cuisines: Wine Bar, Tapas Bar, Sandwiches
Average price: Modest
Area: Ixelles, Chatelain
Address: Rue du Page 34
1050 Brussels, Belgium
Phone: 02 538 96 99

#280
Pataya Restaurant
Cuisines: Belgian, Asian Fusion, Thai
Average price: Modest
Area: Bruxelles, Centre-Ville, Dansaert
Address: Rue Antoine Dansaert 49
1000 Brussels, Belgium
Phone: 02 513 30 57

#281
Au Saint d'Hic
Cuisines: Cafe, Bistro
Average price: Modest
Area: Bruxelles, Centre-Ville, Stalingrad
Address: Place Rouppe 5
1000 Brussels, Belgium
Phone: 02 514 63 13

#282
La Sardine du Marseillais
Cuisines: Sandwiches
Average price: Inexpensive
Area: Bruxelles, Centre-Ville, Marolles
Address: 159 rue Blaes
1000 Brussels, Belgium
Phone: 0487 76 82 98

#283
La Crèmerie de Linkebeek
Cuisines: Cheese Shop, Sandwiches
Average price: Modest
Area: Bruxelles, Centre-Ville, Dansaert
Address: Rue du Vieux Marché aux Grains 4
1000 Brussels, Belgium
Phone: 02 512 35 10

#284
Monya
Cuisines: Moroccan
Average price: Modest
Area: Bruxelles, Centre-Ville
Address: Rue des Hirondelles 9
1000 Brussels, Belgium
Phone: 02 219 89 67

#285
De Bruxelles et d'ailleurs
Cuisines: Belgian
Average price: Modest
Area: Bruxelles, Centre-Ville
Address: Place de la Liberté 13
1000 Brussels, Belgium
Phone: 02 203 26 29

#286
Grimbergen Bruxelles café
Cuisines: Brasserie
Average price: Modest
Area: Bruxelles, Centre-Ville
Address: Place St Catherine 22
1000 Brussels, Belgium
Phone: 02 229 00 09

#287
Tiago's
Cuisines: European
Average price: Expensive
Area: Bruxelles, Quartier Européen
Address: 7 rue Archimède
1000 Brussels, Belgium
Phone: 02 230 00 07

#288
Kokob
Cuisines: Ethiopian, African, Halal
Average price: Expensive
Area: Bruxelles, Centre-Ville, Stalingrad
Address: Rue des Grands Carmes 10
1000 Brussels, Belgium
Phone: 02 511 19 50

#289
Café Métropole
Cuisines: Bar, French
Average price: Expensive
Area: Bruxelles, Centre-Ville, Martyrs
Address: Place de Brouckere 31
1000 Brussels, Belgium
Phone: 02 217 23 00

#290
La Villette
Cuisines: Belgian
Average price: Expensive
Area: Bruxelles, Centre-Ville, Dansaert
Address: Rue du Vieux Marché aux Grains 3
1000 Brussels, Belgium
Phone: 02 512 75 50

#291
Chez Claude
Cuisines: Belgian
Average price: Modest
Area: Bruxelles, Centre-Ville, Dansaert
Address: Rue de Flandre 36
1000 Brussels, Belgium
Phone: 02 511 98 22

#292
Green Lab
Cuisines: Tapas/Small Plates, Cocktail Bar
Average price: Modest
Area: Bruxelles, Louise
Address: Avenue Louise 520
1000 Brussels, Belgium
Phone: 02 644 26 63

#293
L'Idiot du Village
Cuisines: French
Average price: Exclusive
Area: Bruxelles, Centre-Ville, Marolles
Address: Rue Notre-Seigneur 19
1000 Brussels, Belgium
Phone: 02 502 55 82

#294
Le Troisième Acte
Cuisines: Mediterranean, Brasserie
Average price: Expensive
Area: Bruxelles, Centre-Ville, Sablon
Address: Rue Charles Hanssens 6
1000 Brussels, Belgium
Phone: 02 503 56 32

#295
Kamilou
Cuisines: Cafe, Buffet
Average price: Modest
Area: Ixelles, Etangs d'Ixelles
Address: Rue d'Edimbourg 26
1050 Brussels, Belgium
Phone: 0472 44 57 14

#296
La Fabrique en Ville
Cuisines: Coffee & Tea, Breakfast & Brunch
Average price: Expensive
Area: Bruxelles, Centre-Ville, Sablon
Address: Parc d'Egmont, Boulevard de
Waterloo 44
1000 Brussels, Belgium
Phone: 02 513 99 48

#297
Le Paon Royal
Cuisines: Belgian
Average price: Expensive
Area: Bruxelles, Centre-Ville, Dansaert
Address: Rue du Vieux Marché aux Grains 6
1000 Brussels, Belgium
Phone: 02 513 08 68

#298
Zen Kot
Cuisines: Massage, Cafe, Vegetarian
Average price: Modest
Area: Bruxelles, Centre-Ville, Marolles
Address: Rue des Renards 24
1000 Brussels, Belgium
Phone: 02 511 15 11

#299
La Bocca Degli Artisti
Cuisines: Italian
Average price: Modest
Area: Bruxelles, Centre-Ville
Address: Rue de l'Enseignement 104
1000 Brussels, Belgium
Phone: 04 65895857

#300
Yi Chan
Cuisines: Cocktail Bar, Asian Fusion
Average price: Modest
Area: Bruxelles, Centre-Ville, Dansaert
Address: Rue Jules Van Praet 13
1000 Brussels, Belgium
Phone: 02 502 87 66

#301
Chutney's
Cuisines: Brasserie, Belgian, Bar
Average price: Expensive
Area: Bruxelles, Centre-Ville, Quartier Royal
Address: Rue Duquesnoy 5
1000 Brussels, Belgium
Phone: 02 505 55 55

#302
Meyboom
Cuisines: Belgian, Cafe
Average price: Modest
Area: Bruxelles, Centre-Ville, Martyrs
Address: Rue des Sables 39
1000 Brussels, Belgium
Phone: 02 219 55 99

#303
Le Petit Normand
Cuisines: Butcher, Cheese Shop, Sandwiches
Average price: Modest
Area: Bruxelles, Centre-Ville, Dansaert
Address: Rue de Tabora 5
1000 Brussels, Belgium
Phone: 02 513 00 93

#304
Café Central
Cuisines: Bar, Belgian
Average price: Modest
Area: Bruxelles, Centre-Ville, Dansaert
Address: Rue Borgval 14
1000 Brussels, Belgium
Phone: 02 513 73 08

#305
New Rugbyman Numéro 2
Cuisines: Belgian
Average price: Expensive
Area: Bruxelles, Centre-Ville
Address: Quai aux Briques 12
1000 Brussels, Belgium
Phone: 02 512 37 60

#306
Jai Ho
Cuisines: Indian
Average price: Modest
Area: Bruxelles, Centre-Ville
Address: Boulvard Emile Jacqmain 84
1000 Brussels, Belgium
Phone: 04 65713027

#307
La Cigale
Cuisines: French, Convenience Store
Average price: Modest
Area: Bruxelles, Centre-Ville
Address: Rue Saint-Jean 33
1000 Brussels, Belgium
Phone: 0479 95 73 76

#308
Le Chat Noir
Cuisines: Belgian
Average price: Modest
Area: Bruxelles, Centre-Ville, Dansaert
Address: Rue Jules Van Praet 8
1000 Brussels, Belgium
Phone: 02 512 10 77

#309
Le Lotus Bleu
Cuisines: Vietnamese
Average price: Modest
Area: Bruxelles, Centre-Ville, Stalingrad
Address: Rue du Midi 70
1000 Brussels, Belgium
Phone: 02 502 62 99

#310
Rock Classic
Cuisines: Cafe, Bar, Music Venue
Average price: Inexpensive
Area: Bruxelles, Centre-Ville, Stalingrad
Address: Rue du Marché au Charbon 55
1000 Brussels, Belgium
Phone: 02 512 15 47

#311
Standby
Cuisines: Sandwiches, Tapas Bar, Bar
Average price: Modest
Area: Bruxelles, Centre-Ville, Quartier Royal
Address: Rue de Namur 72
1000 Brussels, Belgium
Phone: 02 450 45 11

#312
Atrium
Cuisines: European, Belgian
Average price: Expensive
Area: Bruxelles, Centre-Ville
Address: Rue du Fossé aux Loups 47
1000 Brussels, Belgium
Phone: 02 227 31 70

#313
L'Huîtrière
Cuisines: Belgian, Seafood
Average price: Expensive
Area: Bruxelles, Centre-Ville
Address: Quai aux Briques 20
1000 Brussels, Belgium
Phone: 02 512 08 66

#314
Kafenio
Cuisines: Greek
Average price: Modest
Area: Bruxelles, Quartier Européen
Address: Rue Stevin 134
1000 Brussels, Belgium
Phone: 02 231 55 55

#315
The Food Box
Cuisines: Burgers, Hot Dogs
Average price: Modest
Area: Bruxelles, Centre-Ville
Address: Rue Grétry 47
1000 Brussels, Belgium
Phone: 0485 22 31 33

#316
Plattesteen
Cuisines: Cafe, Belgian
Average price: Modest
Area: Bruxelles, Centre-Ville, Dansaert
Address: Rue du Marché au Charbon 41
1000 Brussels, Belgium
Phone: 02 512 59 92

#317
Café Kafka
Cuisines: Pub, Cafe, Belgian
Average price: Inexpensive
Area: Bruxelles, Centre-Ville, Dansaert
Address: Rue des Poissonniers 21
1000 Brussels, Belgium
Phone: 02 513 66 31

#318
Maxburg Café
Cuisines: German, Cafe, Pub
Average price: Modest
Area: Bruxelles, Quartier Européen
Address: Rue Stevin 108
1000 Brussels, Belgium
Phone: 02 230 22 67

#319
Tout Bon
Cuisines: Breakfast & Brunch, Bakery, Coffee & Tea
Average price: Modest
Area: Ixelles, Quartier Européen
Address: Rue du Luxembourg 68
1000 Brussels, Belgium
Phone: 02 230 42 44

#320
The Meeting Point
Cuisines: Belgian, Pizza, Irish Pub
Average price: Inexpensive
Area: Bruxelles, Quartier Européen
Address: Rue du Taciturne 39
1000 Brussels, Belgium
Phone: 02 230 28 02

#321
Ploegmans
Cuisines: Belgian, Brasserie
Average price: Expensive
Area: Bruxelles, Centre-Ville, Marolles
Address: Hoogstraat 148
1000 Brussels, Belgium
Phone: 02 503 21 24

#322
Brasserie Leopold
Cuisines: Brasserie
Average price: Expensive
Area: Quartier Européen
Address: Rue du Luxembourg 35
1050 Brussels, Belgium
Phone: 02 511 18 28

#323
La Crèmerie de la Vache
Cuisines: Tea Room, Breakfast & Brunch
Average price: Modest
Area: Bruxelles, Saint-Gilles, Louise
Address: Rue Jean Stas 6
1060 Brussels, Belgium
Phone: 02 538 28 18

#324
Mam Mam
Cuisines: Thai
Average price: Modest
Area: Bruxelles, Centre-Ville
Address: Kolenmarkt 72
1000 Brussels, Belgium
Phone: 02 502 00 76

#325
Brasserie Meat Me
Cuisines: Brasserie
Average price: Modest
Area: Bruxelles, Centre-Ville, Martyrs
Address: Bd Adolphe Maxlaan 96
1000 Brussels, Belgium
Phone: 02 227 04 03

#326
La Marmite
Cuisines: Brasserie
Average price: Modest
Area: Bruxelles, Centre-Ville, Marolles
Address: Rue Haute 304
1000 Brussels, Belgium
Phone: 0471 58 27 68

#327
Le Corrège
Cuisines: Belgian, French
Average price: Modest
Area: Bruxelles, Quartier Européen
Address: Rue le Corrège 90
1000 Brussels, Belgium
Phone: 02 734 34 12

#328
La Caneva
Cuisines: Italian
Average price: Modest
Area: Bruxelles, Centre-Ville, Stalingrad
Address: Rue des Grands Carmes 9
1000 Brussels, Belgium
Phone: 02 512 34 47

#329
Restaurant de la Bourse
Cuisines: Belgian
Average price: Modest
Area: Bruxelles, Centre-Ville, Dansaert
Address: Rue de Flandre 32
1000 Brussels, Belgium
Phone: 02 511 99 29

#330
Samouraï
Cuisines: Japanese
Average price: Modest
Area: Bruxelles, Centre-Ville, Martyrs
Address: Rue Fossé aux Loups 28B
1000 Brussels, Belgium
Phone: 02 217 56 39

#331
Thanh-Binh
Cuisines: Vietnamese
Average price: Modest
Area: Bruxelles, Centre-Ville, Dansaert
Address: Rue Jules Van Praet 7
1000 Brussels, Belgium
Phone: 02 513 81 18

#332
Casa Miguel
Cuisines: Spanish, Seafood, Tapas
Average price: Modest
Area: Bruxelles, Quartier Européen
Address: Place des Gueux 2
1000 Brussels, Belgium
Phone: 02 735 41 00

#333
L'Ecailler du Palais Royal
Cuisines: French, Seafood
Average price: Exclusive
Area: Bruxelles, Centre-Ville, Quartier Royal
Address: Rue Bodenbroek 18
1000 Brussels, Belgium
Phone: 02 512 87 51

#334
La Brace
Cuisines: Italian, Pizza
Average price: Modest
Area: Bruxelles, Quartier Européen
Address: Rue Franklin 1
1000 Brussels, Belgium
Phone: 02 736 57 73

#335
Maison des Crêpes
Cuisines: Creperies
Average price: Modest
Area: Bruxelles, Centre-Ville, Dansaert
Address: Rue du Midi 13
1000 Brussels, Belgium
Phone: 0475 95 73 68

#336
Brussels Grill
Cuisines: Steakhouse, Brasserie, American
Average price: Modest
Area: Centre-Ville, Saint-Josse-Ten-Noode
Address: 21 avenue du Boulevard
1210 Brussels, Belgium
Phone: 02 274 13 30

#337
Tasty break
Cuisines: Sandwiches
Average price: Inexpensive
Area: Bruxelles, Centre-Ville, Stalingrad
Address: Rue de l'escalier 6
1000 Brussels, Belgium
Phone: 0485 91 47 55

#338
Park Side
Cuisines: Brasserie
Average price: Modest
Area: Bruxelles, Mérode, Quartier Européen
Address: Avenue de la Joyeuse Entrée 24
1000 Brussels, Belgium
Phone: 02 238 08 08

#339
Kumquat
Cuisines: Vietnamese, Thai
Average price: Modest
Area: Bruxelles, Centre-Ville
Address: Rue du Nord 1
1000 Brussels, Belgium
Phone: 02 514 14 80

#340
Zebra Bar
Cuisines: Cafe, Bar, Coffee & Tea
Average price: Modest
Area: Bruxelles, Centre-Ville, Dansaert
Address: Place Saint-Géry 33
1000 Brussels, Belgium
Phone: 02 503 43 00

#341
Au Bon Vieux Temps
Cuisines: Cafe
Average price: Modest
Area: Bruxelles, Centre-Ville, Grand-Place
Address: Impasse Saint-Nicolas 4
1000 Brussels, Belgium
Phone: 02 217 26 26

#342
L'Apèro
Cuisines: Bar, Bistro
Average price: Modest
Area: Bruxelles, Centre-Ville, Martyrs
Address: Rue du Marais 1
1000 Brussels, Belgium
Phone: 02 206 06 87

#343
Brussels Grill
Cuisines: Steakhouse, Barbeque, Belgian
Average price: Modest
Area: Bruxelles, Centre-Ville, Martyrs
Address: Place De Brouckère 19
1000 Brussels, Belgium
Phone: 02 219 12 19

#344
Au Bon Bol
Cuisines: Chinese
Average price: Modest
Area: Bruxelles, Centre-Ville, Dansaert
Address: Rue Paul Devaux 9
1000 Brussels, Belgium
Phone: 02 513 16 88

#345
Restaurant du Mim
Cuisines: Belgian
Average price: Expensive
Area: Bruxelles, Centre-Ville, Quartier Royal
Address: Rue Montagne de la Cour 2
1000 Brussels, Belgium
Phone: 02 502 95 08

#346
Los Churros
Cuisines: Donuts, Cafeteria
Average price: Inexpensive
Area: Bruxelles, Centre-Ville, Grand-Place
Address: Rue de Tabora 4
1000 Brussels, Belgium
Phone: 02 514 94 09

#347
Letiuz Salad Bar
Cuisines: Salad
Average price: Modest
Area: Bruxelles, Quartier Européen
Address: Rue de l'industrie 4
1000 Brussels, Belgium
Phone: 02 512 32 22

#348
Le Grand Café
Cuisines: Bar, Belgian
Average price: Modest
Area: Bruxelles, Centre-Ville, Dansaert
Address: Boulevard Anspach 78
1000 Brussels, Belgium
Phone: 02 513 02 03

#349
Break Time
Cuisines: Sandwiches
Average price: Inexpensive
Area: Bruxelles, Porte De Namur
Address: Ave Marnix 14C
1000 Brussels, Belgium
Phone: 02 502 01 23

#350
Brussels Grill Grand Place Brussels
Cuisines: Belgian, Steakhouse
Average price: Modest
Area: Bruxelles, Centre-Ville, Grand-Place
Address: Rue Marché aux Herbes 89
1000 Brussels, Belgium
Phone: 02 503 17 22

#351
Divino
Cuisines: Italian, Pizza
Average price: Modest
Area: Bruxelles, Centre-Ville, Dansaert
Address: Rue Des Chartreux 56
1000 Brussels, Belgium
Phone: 02 503 39 09

#352
La Cantine de l'Atelier des Tanneurs
Cuisines: Buffet
Average price: Expensive
Area: Bruxelles, Centre-Ville, Marolles
Address: Rue des Tanneurs 58-62
1000 Brussels, Belgium
Phone: 02 548 70 40

#353
La Villa Emily
Cuisines: French
Average price: Exclusive
Area: Ixelles, Bruxelles, La Bascule
Address: Rue de l'Abbaye 4
1000 Brussels, Belgium
Phone: 02 318 18 58

#354
Osteria Pane e Vino
Cuisines: Italian, Fast Food
Average price: Modest
Area: Bruxelles, Quartier Européen
Address: Rue Archimède 48
1000 Brussels, Belgium
Phone: 02 230 59 51

#355
La Rotonde
Cuisines: Brasserie
Average price: Expensive
Area: Bruxelles, Centre-Ville
Address: Rue de l'Enseignement 1
1000 Brussels, Belgium
Phone: 02 219 64 10

#356
Pasta Queen
Cuisines: Italian
Average price: Inexpensive
Area: Bruxelles, Centre-Ville
Address: Rue de l'Ecuyer 59
1000 Brussels, Belgium
Phone: 02 502 36 43

#357
El Metteko
Cuisines: Cafe
Average price: Modest
Area: Bruxelles, Centre-Ville, Dansaert
Address: Boulevard Anspach 88
1000 Brussels, Belgium
Phone: 02 512 46 48

#358
Comics Cafe
Cuisines: Brasserie, Comic Books
Average price: Expensive
Area: Bruxelles, Centre-Ville, Quartier Royal
Address: Place du Grand Sablon 8
1000 Brussels, Belgium
Phone: 02 513 13 23

#359
Exki
Cuisines: Sandwiches, Salad
Average price: Modest
Area: Bruxelles, Centre-Ville
Address: Place De Brouckère 14
1000 Brussels, Belgium
Phone: 02 219 98 55

#360
Brasserie De La Presse
Cuisines: Brasserie
Average price: Expensive
Area: Bruxelles, Centre-Ville
Address: Rue Royale 100
1000 Brussels, Belgium
Phone: 02 201 50 85

#361
Ebrius Artis Bar
Cuisines: Bar, Cafe, Music Venue
Average price: Inexpensive
Area: Bruxelles, Centre-Ville, Stalingrad
Address: Place Rouppe 6
1000 Brussels, Belgium
Phone: 0485 68 74 06

#362
Tarte Julie
Cuisines: Bakery, Cafe, Pizza
Average price: Inexpensive
Area: Bruxelles, Centre-Ville
Address: Boulevard Emile Jacqmain 56
1000 Brussels, Belgium
Phone: 02 218 53 89

#363
Le Plattsteen
Cuisines: Cafe
Average price: Modest
Area: Bruxelles, Centre-Ville, Dansaert
Address: Rue du Marché au Charbon 41
1000 Brussels, Belgium
Phone: 02 512 82 03

#364
La Tortue du Sablon
Cuisines: Barbeque, Seafood, Belgian
Average price: Expensive
Area: Bruxelles, Centre-Ville, Marolles
Address: Rue de Rollebeek 31
1000 Brussels, Belgium
Phone: 02 513 10 62

#365
Le Food Factory
Cuisines: Bar, Belgian
Average price: Modest
Area: Bruxelles, Centre-Ville
Address: Bd Anspach 37
1000 Brussels, Belgium
Phone: 02 229 32 80

#366
Chez Richard
Cuisines: Cafe
Average price: Modest
Area: Bruxelles, Centre-Ville, Sablon
Address: Rue des Minimes 2
1000 Brussels, Belgium
Phone: 02 512 14 06

#367
Bocconi
Cuisines: Italian
Average price: Expensive
Area: Bruxelles, Centre-Ville, Dansaert
Address: Rue de l'Amigo 1
1000 Brussels, Belgium
Phone: 02 547 47 15

#368
Le Belgo Thai
Cuisines: Brasserie, Thai
Average price: Expensive
Area: Bruxelles, Centre-Ville, Marolles
Address: Rue Haute 72
1000 Brussels, Belgium
Phone: 02 808 40 88

#369
Natural caffè Bourse
Cuisines: Salad, Coffee & Tea, Sandwiches
Average price: Inexpensive
Area: Bruxelles, Centre-Ville, Dansaert
Address: Boulevard Anspach 66
1000 Brussels, Belgium
Phone: 02 513 26 63

#370
Centro Cabraliego
Cuisines: Spanish
Average price: Inexpensive
Area: Bruxelles, Centre-Ville, Marolles
Address: Rue Haute 171
1000 Brussels, Belgium
Phone: 02 511 05 59

#371
Restauration Roumaine
Cuisines: Romanian, Belgian
Average price: Modest
Area: Bruxelles, Centre-Ville
Address: Rue Gretry 13
1000 Brussels, Belgium
Phone: 0474 26 17 48

#372
Vespa Caffè
Cuisines: Italian, Sandwiches
Average price: Modest
Area: Bruxelles, Quartier Européen
Address: Rue Joseph II 19
1000 Brussels, Belgium
Phone: 0488 65 01 99

#373
Attica Restaurant
Cuisines: Sandwiches, Burgers, Greek
Average price: Inexpensive
Area: Bruxelles, Quartier Européen
Address: Rue de Treves 49 - 51
1000 Brussels, Belgium
Phone: 02 280 29 00

#374
Citron Vert
Cuisines: Thai
Average price: Modest
Area: Bruxelles, Centre-Ville
Address: Rue de l'Enseignement 116
1000 Brussels, Belgium
Phone: 02 218 54 00

#375
L'huile sur Le Feu
Cuisines: Mediterranean
Average price: Expensive
Area: Mérode, Etterbeek
Address: Rue de Linthout 242
1040 Brussels, Belgium
Phone: 02 734 96 00

#376
Menelas
Cuisines: Belgian
Average price: Modest
Area: Bruxelles, Centre-Ville, Dansaert
Address: Rue du Vieux Marche aux Grains
25, 1000 Brussels, Belgium
Phone: 02 512 67 39

#377
Café De Markten
Cuisines: Bar, Music Venue, Sandwiches
Average price: Modest
Area: Bruxelles, Centre-Ville, Dansaert
Address: Rue du Vieux Marché aux Grains 5
1000 Brussels, Belgium
Phone: 02 513 98 55

#378
Au P'tit Breton
Cuisines: Creperies
Average price: Modest
Area: Ixelles, Chatelain
Address: Rue Américaine 117
1050 Brussels, Belgium
Phone: 02 534 00 08

#379
Chez Martin
Cuisines: Italian
Average price: Modest
Area: Bruxelles, Centre-Ville, Dansaert
Address: Rue Borgwal 17
1000 Brussels, Belgium
Phone: 02 513 93 03

#380
O Reilly's
Cuisines: Irish Pub, Pub, Irish
Average price: Modest
Area: Bruxelles, Centre-Ville, Dansaert
Address: Place de la Bourse 1
1000 Brussels, Belgium
Phone: 02 552 04 81

#381
Zanzibar
Cuisines: French, Fast Food, European
Average price: Inexpensive
Area: Bruxelles, Centre-Ville, Marolles
Address: Rue Haute 318
1000 Brussels, Belgium
Phone: 02 534 76 76

#382
Baan Chann
Cuisines: Thai
Average price: Modest
Area: Saint-Gilles
Address: Rue de Savoie 13
1060 Brussels, Belgium
Phone: 02 534 50 01

#383
Artipasta
Cuisines: Art Gallery, Italian
Average price: Modest
Area: Bruxelles, Centre-Ville
Address: Place de la Liberté 1
1000 Brussels, Belgium
Phone: 02 217 07 37

#384
Les Crustacés
Cuisines: Seafood
Average price: Modest
Area: Bruxelles, Centre-Ville
Address: Quai aux Briques 8
1000 Brussels, Belgium
Phone: 02 513 14 93

#385
Lunch Garden
Cuisines: Belgian
Average price: Modest
Area: Bruxelles, Centre-Ville, Martyrs
Address: Nieuwstraat 111
1000 Brussels, Belgium
Phone: 02 219 35 79

#386
Suki Noodles
Cuisines: Japanese
Average price: Modest
Area: Bruxelles, Centre-Ville
Address: Rue Paul Delvaux 4
1000 Brussels, Belgium
Phone: 02 512 83 71

#387
La Chaloupe d'or
Cuisines: French, Belgian
Average price: Expensive
Area: Bruxelles, Centre-Ville, Grand-Place
Address: Grand-Place 24-25
1000 Brussels, Belgium
Phone: 02 511 41 61

#388
Au Lotus Thaï
Cuisines: Thai
Average price: Modest
Area: Bruxelles, Centre-Ville, Dansaert
Address: Rue Jules Van Praet 31
1000 Brussels, Belgium
Phone: 02 502 07 29

#389
Le Forestier
Cuisines: Cafe
Average price: Modest
Area: Bruxelles, Centre-Ville, Marolles
Address: Rue Haute 2
1000 Brussels, Belgium
Phone: 02 513 72 97

#390
Il Ramo Verdee
Cuisines: Italian
Average price: Expensive
Area: Bruxelles, Quartier Européen
Address: Rue de Toulouse 46
1040 Brussels, Belgium
Phone: 02 280 65 47

#391
Le P'tit Chouia En +
Cuisines: Moroccan
Average price: Inexpensive
Area: Bruxelles
Address: Rue de la Pacification 38
1000 Brussels, Belgium
Phone: 02 230 70 25

#392
IIT Molto Tasty
Cuisines: Fast Food, Italian
Average price: Inexpensive
Area: Bruxelles, Centre-Ville, Martyrs
Address: Bd Emile Jacqmain 137
1000 Brussels, Belgium
Phone: 02 201 11 23

#393
Cap d'Argent, Taverne
Cuisines: Cafe
Average price: Modest
Area: Bruxelles, Centre-Ville, Quartier Royal
Address: Rue Ravenstein 10
1000 Brussels, Belgium
Phone: 02 513 09 19

#394
Il Vecchio Mulino
Cuisines: Italian, Pizza
Average price: Modest
Area: Saint-Gilles, Louise
Address: Rue Jourdan 60
1060 Brussels, Belgium
Phone: 02 534 44 19

#395
**Novotel Bruxelles Centre
Tour Noire**
Cuisines: Cafe, Hotel, Day Spa
Average price: Exclusive
Area: Bruxelles, Centre-Ville
Address: Rue de la Vierge Noire 32
1000 Brussels, Belgium
Phone: 02 505 50 50

#396
Little Asia
Cuisines: Vietnamese
Average price: Exclusive
Area: Bruxelles, Centre-Ville, Dansaert
Address: Rue Sainte-Catherine 8
1000 Brussels, Belgium
Phone: 02 502 88 36

#397
Shao Shan
Cuisines: Dim Sum, Buffet
Average price: Modest
Area: Bruxelles, Centre-Ville, Martyrs
Address: Warmoesberg 49
1000 Brussels, Belgium
Phone: 02 219 04 21

#398
EL Bocadillo
Cuisines: Coffee & Tea,
Breakfast & Brunch, Sandwiches
Average price: Modest
Area: Bruxelles, Centre-Ville
Address: Rue de Laeken 2
1000 Brussels, Belgium
Phone: 02 223 33 46

#399
Sultans of Kébab
Cuisines: Turkish
Average price: Inexpensive
Area: Bruxelles, Centre-Ville
Address: Boulevard Anspach 49
1000 Brussels, Belgium
Phone: 02 201 10 32

#400
Kabuki
Cuisines: Sushi Bar, Japanese
Average price: Expensive
Area: Bruxelles, Centre-Ville
Address: Rue du Marché aux Poulets 32
1000 Brussels, Belgium
Phone: 02 218 86 96

#401
Brasserie du Gourmet
Cuisines: French, Brasserie
Average price: Expensive
Area: Bruxelles, Centre-Ville
Address: Place du Béguinage 6
1000 Brussels, Belgium
Phone: 02 223 33 40

#402
Drug Opera
Cuisines: Brasserie, Belgian, Cafe
Average price: Modest
Area: Bruxelles, Centre-Ville
Address: Rue Grétry 51
1000 Brussels, Belgium
Phone: 02 229 16 66

#403
La Natura
Cuisines: Breakfast & Brunch,
Italian, Sandwiches
Average price: Inexpensive
Area: Bruxelles, Centre-Ville, Martyrs
Address: Rue du Marais 13
1000 Brussels, Belgium
Phone: 0487 32 18 24

#404
Le Pain Bénit
Cuisines: Belgian, Sandwiches
Average price: Inexpensive
Area: Ixelles, Bruxelles, Chatelain
Address: Rue du Bailli 12
1000 Brussels, Belgium
Phone: 02 649 93 66

#405
Madou's Folie
Cuisines: French, Belgian,
Event Planning & Service
Average price: Expensive
Area: Bruxelles, Centre-Ville
Address: Rue de la Presse 23
1000 Brussels, Belgium
Phone: 02 217 38 31

#406
Osteria Agricola
Cuisines: Italian
Average price: Expensive
Area: Bruxelles, Quartier Européen
Address: Avenue Livingstone 20
1000 Brussels, Belgium
Phone: 02 231 64 07

#407
Pulp
Cuisines: Sandwiches
Average price: Inexpensive
Area: Bruxelles, Quartier Européen
Address: 16 rue Archimède
1040 Brussels, Belgium
Phone: 02 513 50 16

#408
Les Tropiques
Cuisines: African
Average price: Modest
Area: Bruxelles, Centre-Ville, Marolles
Address: Rue aux Laines 43
1000 Brussels, Belgium
Phone: 0488 41 55 83

#409
KWINT
Cuisines: French, Lounge
Average price: Expensive
Area: Bruxelles, Centre-Ville, Quartier Royal
Address: Mont des Arts 1
1000 Brussels, Belgium
Phone: 02 505 95 95

#410
Dominican Lounge
Cuisines: African, Belgian
Average price: Expensive
Area: Bruxelles, Centre-Ville
Address: Rue Leopold 9
1000 Brussels, Belgium
Phone: 02 203 08 08

#411
Cosy Corner
Cuisines: Fast Food, Vegetarian
Average price: Inexpensive
Area: Bruxelles, Centre-Ville, Anneesens
Address: Boulevard Maurice Lemonnier 49-51, 1000 Brussels, Belgium
Phone: 0488 83 16 35

#412
La Truffe Noire
Cuisines: European
Average price: Exclusive
Area: Bruxelles
Address: Bd de la Cambre 12
1000 Brussels, Belgium
Phone: 02 640 44 22

#413
La Crêperie
Cuisines: Creperies
Average price: Modest
Area: Bruxelles, Centre-Ville, Marolles
Address: Rue Haute 35
1000 Brussels, Belgium
Phone: 0489 68 72 23

#414
Il Gallo Nero
Cuisines: Italian
Average price: Modest
Area: Bruxelles, Quartier Européen
Address: Rue Franklin 21
1000 Brussels, Belgium
Phone: 02 734 13 11

#415
Eat Sushi
Cuisines: Japanese, Sushi Bar
Average price: Modest
Area: Ixelles, Porte De Namur
Address: Place du Champ de Mars 5
1050 Brussels, Belgium
Phone: 02 207 15 70

#416
Oysters and Smorrebrod
Cuisines: Seafood, Sandwiches
Average price: Modest
Area: Bruxelles, Centre-Ville
Address: Place Sainte-Catherine 49
1000 Brussels, Belgium
Phone: 0494 04 01 80

#417
Mamma Roma
Cuisines: Pizza
Average price: Modest
Area: Bruxelles, Centre-Ville, Dansaert
Address: Rue du Pont de la Carpe 17
1000 Brussels, Belgium
Phone: 02 502 13 03

#418
POP UP Sablon
Cuisines: Brasserie, Belgian, Bar
Average price: Expensive
Area: Bruxelles, Centre-Ville, Quartier Royal
Address: Place du Grand Sablon 15 16
1000 Brussels, Belgium
Phone: 02 503 65 70

#419
La Péniche
Cuisines: Bar, Bistro
Average price: Inexpensive
Area: Bruxelles, Centre-Ville
Address: Quai au Bois à Brûler 37
1000 Brussels, Belgium
Phone: 02 219 13 93

#420
Le Pain De France
Cuisines: Salad, Sandwiches
Average price: Inexpensive
Area: Bruxelles, Centre-Ville, Quartier Royal
Address: Galerie Ravenstein, 52
1000 Brussels, Belgium
Phone: 0478 21 77 54

#421
Chili
Cuisines: Cocktail Bar, Tapas Bar
Average price: Modest
Area: Bruxelles, Centre-Ville, Dansaert
Address: Place Saint-Géry 1
1000 Brussels, Belgium
Phone: 0487 56 46 14

#422
Pizza Bella
Cuisines: Italian
Average price: Modest
Area: Bruxelles, Quartier Européen
Address: Rue Joseph II 15a
1000 Brussels, Belgium
Phone: 02 230 32 37

#423
Greenhouse
Cuisines: Brasserie
Average price: Expensive
Area: Bruxelles, Saint-Gilles, Louise
Address: Avenue Louise 43
1050 Brussels, Belgium
Phone: 02 537 40 24

#424
Le Cap
Cuisines: Bar, Brasserie
Average price: Expensive
Area: Bruxelles, Centre-Ville, Stalingrad
Address: Place de la Vieille Halle aux Blès 28
1000 Brussels, Belgium
Phone: 02 512 93 42

#425
Bon Luxembourg
Cuisines: Juice Bar, Sandwiches
Average price: Modest
Area: Bruxelles, Quartier Européen
Address: Rue du Luxembourg 23
1000 Brussels, Belgium
Phone: 02 514 37 07

#426
L'Atelier de la Truffe Noire
Cuisines: European
Average price: Exclusive
Area: Ixelles, Bruxelles, Etangs d'Ixelles
Address: Avenue Louise 300
1000 Brussels, Belgium
Phone: 02 640 54 55

#427
Bombay Inn
Cuisines: Indian
Average price: Modest
Area: Bruxelles, Centre-Ville
Address: Rue de la Fourche 38
1000 Brussels, Belgium
Phone: 02 219 59 54

#428
Chez Jacques
Cuisines: Seafood
Average price: Modest
Area: Bruxelles, Centre-Ville
Address: Quais aux Briques 44
1000 Brussels, Belgium
Phone: 02 512 20 27

#429
Et qui va ramener le chien?
Cuisines: European, Belgian, French
Average price: Expensive
Area: Bruxelles, Centre-Ville, Marolles
Address: Rue de Rollebeek 2
1000 Brussels, Belgium
Phone: 02 503 23 04

#430
Casa Mia
Cuisines: Italian
Average price: Modest
Area: Bruxelles, Quartier Européen
Address: Rue de la loi 28
1000 Brussels, Belgium
Phone: 02 280 03 68

#431
Annapurna
Cuisines: Indian
Average price: Modest
Area: Bruxelles, Centre-Ville
Address: Rue de Laeken 26
1000 Brussels, Belgium
Phone: 02 219 39 33

#432
Le Routier - Emile Bistro
Cuisines: Sandwiches, Bistro
Average price: Inexpensive
Area: Ixelles
Address: Avenue Emile De Beco 22
1000 Brussels, Belgium
Phone: 02 642 96 29

#433
Todt's Café
Cuisines: Brasserie, Bar, Local Flavor
Average price: Modest
Area: Bruxelles, Centre-Ville, Marolles
Address: Rue de Rollebeek 11
1000 Brussels, Belgium
Phone: 02 502 77 83

#434
Charli
Cuisines: Sandwiches, Bakery
Average price: Modest
Area: Bruxelles, Centre-Ville
Address: Rue Sainte Catherine 34
1000 Brussels, Belgium
Phone: 02 502 05 15

#435
Hong Kong Delight
Cuisines: Chinese
Average price: Modest
Area: Bruxelles, Centre-Ville, Dansaert
Address: Rue sainte Catherine 35
1000 Brussels, Belgium
Phone: 02 503 26 28

#436
Le Petrus
Cuisines: French
Average price: Modest
Area: Bruxelles, Centre-Ville
Address: Place du Samedi 14
1000 Brussels, Belgium
Phone: 02 219 25 08

#437
Muntpunt Grand Café
Cuisines: Bar, Cafe
Average price: Modest
Area: Bruxelles, Centre-Ville
Address: Rue Léopold 2
1000 Brussels, Belgium
Phone: 02 218 39 18

#438
RUE Royale
Cuisines: Sandwiches
Average price: Inexpensive
Area: Bruxelles, Centre-Ville
Address: Rue Royale 9
1000 Brussels, Belgium
Phone: 02 203 71 11

#439
Le pain de l'Abbaye
Cuisines: Sandwiches
Average price: Modest
Area: Bruxelles, Centre-Ville
Address: Rue Royale 129
1000 Brussels, Belgium
Phone: 02 219 19 88

#440
La Lunette
Cuisines: Cafe
Average price: Modest
Area: Bruxelles, Centre-Ville
Address: Place de la Monnaie 3
1000 Brussels, Belgium
Phone: 02 218 03 78

#441
La Fabbrica
Cuisines: Breakfast & Brunch,
Venue & Event Space, Brasserie
Average price: Modest
Area: Bruxelles, Quartier Maritime
Address: Ave du Port 86
1000 Brussels, Belgium
Phone: 02 428 50 26

#442
Exki
Cuisines: Sandwiches, Salad
Average price: Modest
Area: Bruxelles, Centre-Ville, Martyrs
Address: Rue Neuve 78
1000 Brussels, Belgium
Phone: 02 219 19 91

#443
Sultans of Kebap
Cuisines: Turkish, Fast Food
Average price: Inexpensive
Area: Bruxelles, Centre-Ville, Dansaert
Address: Boulevard Anspach 72
1000 Brussels, Belgium
Phone: 02 201 10 32

#444
Yuka Espresso Bar
Cuisines: Cafe
Average price: Inexpensive
Area: Bruxelles, Centre-Ville, Stalingrad
Address: Boulevard Anspach 166
1000 Brussels, Belgium
Phone: 0477 35 04 06

#445
Palais du Cèdre
Cuisines: Lebanese
Average price: Modest
Area: Bruxelles, Centre-Ville
Address: Rue de l'Enseignement 27
1000 Brussels, Belgium
Phone: 02 217 03 27

#446
Gourmets Every-day
Cuisines: Chinese, Asian Fusion
Average price: Modest
Area: Bruxelles, Centre-Ville, Dansaert
Address: Rue des Poissonniers 11
1000 Brussels, Belgium
Phone: 02 511 86 88

#447
Gaufre de Bruxelles
Cuisines: Creperies, Tea Room, Ice Cream
Average price: Modest
Area: Bruxelles, Centre-Ville, Grand-Place
Address: Grasmarkt 113
1000 Brussels, Belgium
Phone: 02 514 01 71

#448
Kasbah
Cuisines: Moroccan
Average price: Expensive
Area: Bruxelles, Centre-Ville, Dansaert
Address: Rue Antoine Dansaert 20B
1000 Brussels, Belgium
Phone: 02 502 40 26

#449
Brasserie- Restaurant Horta
Cuisines: Brasserie
Average price: Modest
Area: Bruxelles, Centre-Ville, Martyrs
Address: Rue des Sables 20
1000 Brussels, Belgium
Phone: 0495 80 08 05

#450
Restaurant Libanais Faraya
Cuisines: Cafe
Average price: Modest
Area: Bruxelles, Centre-Ville
Address: Rue du Nord 60
1000 Brussels, Belgium
Phone: 02 219 94 16

#451
Manola
Cuisines: Thai
Average price: Modest
Area: Bruxelles, Centre-Ville
Address: Rue de la Croix De Fer 72
1000 Brussels, Belgium
Phone: 02 217 28 00

#452
Brueghel
Cuisines: Belgian
Average price: Expensive
Area: Bruxelles, Centre-Ville
Address: 26 rue des Bouchers
1000 Brussels, Belgium
Phone: 02 502 83 91

#453
La Barcamoule
Cuisines: Seafood, Belgian
Average price: Expensive
Area: Bruxelles, Centre-Ville
Address: Quai au Bois à Brûler 27
1000 Brussels, Belgium
Phone: 02 218 49 97

#454
Shinwi
Cuisines: Asian Fusion, Chinese, Thai
Average price: Modest
Area: Bruxelles, Centre-Ville, Anneesens
Address: Bd Maurice Lemonnier 159
1000 Brussels, Belgium
Phone: 0488 11 82 18

#455
La Porte des Indes
Cuisines: Indian
Average price: Exclusive
Area: Ixelles, Bruxelles, Louise
Address: Avenue Louise 455
1050 Brussels, Belgium
Phone: 02 647 86 51

#456
La Bottega
Cuisines: Italian
Average price: Expensive
Area: Bruxelles, Centre-Ville
Address: rue de l'Enseignement 35-37
1000 Brussels, Belgium
Phone: 02 219 92 00

#457
La Capannina
Cuisines: Cafe
Average price: Expensive
Area: Bruxelles, Centre-Ville, Grand-Place
Address: Petite rue au Beurre 12
1000 Brussels, Belgium
Phone: 02 512 05 45

#458
Au Cochon d'Or
Cuisines: Seafood, Belgian
Average price: Expensive
Area: Bruxelles, Centre-Ville
Address: Quai au bois à bruler 15
1000 Brussels, Belgium
Phone: 02 219 01 19

#459
Sanh-Kee
Cuisines: Asian Fusion
Average price: Modest
Area: Bruxelles, Centre-Ville, Dansaert
Address: Rue Sainte Catherine 22
1000 Brussels, Belgium
Phone: 02 511 02 88

#460
Le Second Degré
Cuisines: Italian
Average price: Exclusive
Area: Bruxelles
Address: 15 ave Legrand
1000 Brussels, Belgium
Phone: 02 647 29 47

#461
Taverne Brosella
Cuisines: Bar, Italian
Average price: Modest
Area: Bruxelles, Centre-Ville, Martyrs
Address: Rue Saint-Michel 36
1000 Brussels, Belgium
Phone: 02 225 36 94

#462
I Primi Piatti
Cuisines: Italian, Pizza
Average price: Modest
Area: Bruxelles, Centre-Ville, Dansaert
Address: Rue de Flandre 26
1000 Brussels, Belgium
Phone: 02 511 79 43

#463
Garden City
Cuisines: Brasserie
Average price: Modest
Area: Bruxelles, Centre-Ville
Address: Place de la Liberté 6
1000 Brussels, Belgium
Phone: 02 734 40 41

#464
Table de Mus
Cuisines: French
Average price: Expensive
Area: Bruxelles, Centre-Ville, Stalingrad
Address: Place de la Vieille Halle aux Blés 31
1000 Brussels, Belgium
Phone: 02 511 05 86

#465
Aksum
Cuisines: Cafe
Average price: Inexpensive
Area: Bruxelles, Centre-Ville, Quartier Royal
Address: Rue des Éperonniers 60
1000 City of Brussels, Belgium
Phone: 02 25112304

#466
Pampas Rodizio
Cuisines: Barbeque, Argentine, Brazilian
Average price: Expensive
Area: Bruxelles, Centre-Ville
Address: Place Sainte-Catherine 15
1000 Brussels, Belgium
Phone: 02 217 90 12

#467
Balthazar
Cuisines: Cafe
Average price: Inexpensive
Area: Bruxelles, Quartier Européen
Address: Rue Archimède 63
1000 Brussels, Belgium
Phone: 02 742 06 00

#468
Chez Saly
Cuisines: Thai
Average price: Expensive
Area: Ixelles, Chatelain
Address: Rue de Livourne 131
1000 Brussels, Belgium
Phone: 02 646 03 10

#469
Bleu de Toi
Cuisines: Cafe
Average price: Expensive
Area: Bruxelles, Centre-Ville, Stalingrad
Address: Rue des Alexiens 73
1000 Brussels, Belgium
Phone: 02 502 43 71

#470
Hotel Orts Café
Cuisines: Bar, Belgian, Hotel
Average price: Modest
Area: Bruxelles, Centre-Ville, Dansaert
Address: Rue Auguste Orts 38-40
1000 Brussels, Belgium
Phone: 02 450 22 00

#471
À L'Apocalypse
Cuisines: Thai, Asian Fusion, Vietnamese
Average price: Modest
Area: Ixelles, Petite Suisse, Université
Address: Chaussée de Boondael 347
1050 Brussels, Belgium
Phone: 02 640 70 95

#472
Etiquette
Cuisines: Tapas Bar, Wine Bar, Delicatessen
Average price: Expensive
Area: Bruxelles
Address: Avenue Emile de Mot 19
1000 Brussels, Belgium
Phone: 02 644 64 11

#473
Il Colosseo
Cuisines: Italian, Pizza
Average price: Modest
Area: Bruxelles, Centre-Ville
Address: Bd Emile Jacqmain 74
1000 Brussels, Belgium
Phone: 02 217 80 05

#474
Sawad
Cuisines: Indian
Average price: Modest
Area: Bruxelles
Address: Chaussée d'Anvers 33
1000 Brussels, Belgium
Phone: 02 201 34 84

#475
Rugantino
Cuisines: Italian
Average price: Modest
Area: Bruxelles, Centre-Ville, Stalingrad
Address: Bd Anspach 184
1000 Brussels, Belgium
Phone: 02 511 21 95

#476
Le Père Tranquille
Cuisines: Belgian, Breakfast & Brunch
Average price: Modest
Area: Bruxelles, Centre-Ville, Marolles
Address: Rue des Renards 1C
1000 Brussels, Belgium
Phone: 0475 49 87 22

#477
Azeb Café
Cuisines: Ethiopian, Cocktail Bar, African
Average price: Modest
Area: Bruxelles, Centre-Ville
Address: Rue du Gouvernement Provisoire
43, 1000 Brussels, Belgium
Phone: 0495 76 87 85

#478
Pizzeria Napoli
Cuisines: Pizza
Average price: Modest
Area: Bruxelles, Centre-Ville
Address: Rue de l'Enseignement 66-68
1000 Brussels, Belgium
Phone: 02 223 70 63

#479
La Capranica
Cuisines: Cafe
Average price: Modest
Area: Bruxelles, Quartier Européen
Address: Avenue Michel-Ange 85
1000 Brussels, Belgium
Phone: 02 736 18 70

#480
Tartine et Moi et Pâtes et Vous
Cuisines: European, Sandwiches, Fast Food
Average price: Modest
Area: Saint-Josse-Ten-Noode
Address: Rue Froissart 137-139
1000 Brussels, Belgium
Phone: 02 280 41 00

#481
YùMe
Cuisines: Brasserie
Average price: Exclusive
Area: Woluwé-Saint-Pierre
Address: Avenue de Tervuren 292
1150 Brussels, Belgium
Phone: 02 773 00 80

#482
Le Corbier
Cuisines: Barbeque
Average price: Expensive
Area: Bruxelles, Centre-Ville, Marolles
Address: Rue des Minimes 51
1000 Brussels, Belgium
Phone: 02 513 51 95

#483
Muntpunt Grand Cafe
Cuisines: Cafe
Average price: Modest
Area: Bruxelles, Centre-Ville
Address: Munt 6
1000 Brussels, Belgium
Phone: 02 278 11 11

#484
Le Grain de Sable
Cuisines: Brasserie, Bistro, Pub
Average price: Expensive
Area: Bruxelles, Centre-Ville, Quartier Royal
Address: Place du Grand Sablon 16-17
1000 Brussels, Belgium
Phone: 02 513 18 41

#485
Bazaar
Cuisines: Dance Club, Music Venue
Average price: Modest
Area: Bruxelles, Centre-Ville, Marolles
Address: Rue des Capucins 63
1000 Brussels, Belgium
Phone: 02 511 26 00

#486
L'Herbaudière
Cuisines: Belgian, Creperies
Average price: Inexpensive
Area: Bruxelles, Centre-Ville
Address: Place de la Liberté 9
1000 Brussels, Belgium
Phone: 02 218 77 13

#487
Le Petit Chou de Bruxelles
Cuisines: Belgian
Average price: Expensive
Area: Bruxelles, Centre-Ville, Dansaert
Address: Rue du Vieux Marché aux Grains
2/A, 1000 Brussels, Belgium
Phone: 02 502 60 37

#488
Leopold
Cuisines: Coffee & Tea,
Bagels, Breakfast & Brunch
Average price: Modest
Area: Etterbeek
Address: Avenue de Tervueren 107
1040 Brussels, Belgium
Phone: 02 736 22 98

#489
Orphyse Chaussette
Cuisines: French
Average price: Exclusive
Area: Bruxelles, Centre-Ville
Address: Rue Charles Hanssens 5
1000 Brussels, Belgium
Phone: 02 502 75 81

#490
Bia Mara
Cuisines: Fish & Chips, Seafood
Average price: Modest
Area: Bruxelles, Centre-Ville, Dansaert
Address: Rue du marché aux poulets 41
1000 City of Brussels, Belgium
Phone: 02 502 00 61

#491
Borsalino
Cuisines: Bar, Italian
Average price: Modest
Area: Ixelles
Address: Ave de la Couronne 73
1050 Brussels, Belgium
Phone: 02 852 56 19

#492
Le Grand Bi
Cuisines: Belgian
Average price: Expensive
Area: Bruxelles, Centre-Ville, Grand-Place
Address: Petite Rue des Bouchers 2
1000 Brussels, Belgium
Phone: 02 511 98 59

#493
Pizzeria Pronto
Cuisines: Italian, Pizza
Average price: Modest
Area: Bruxelles, Centre-Ville, Dansaert
Address: Kiekenmarkt 57
1000 Brussels, Belgium
Phone: 02 511 06 66

#494
Loui Bar
Cuisines: Tapas Bar
Average price: Exclusive
Area: Bruxelles, Louise
Address: 77 ave Louise
1050 Brussels, Belgium
Phone: 02 542 48 37

#495
La Patinoire
Cuisines: Brasserie
Average price: Expensive
Area: Bruxelles, Bois de la Cambre
Address: Chemin du Gymnase 1
1000 Brussels, Belgium
Phone: 02 649 70 02

#496
ABrussel
Cuisines: Belgian, European
Average price: Expensive
Area: Bruxelles, Centre-Ville, Grand-Place
Address: Rue des Chapeliers 34
1000 Brussels, Belgium
Phone: 02 649 01 19

#497
Café Capitale
Cuisines: Cafe, Desserts, Coffee & Tea
Average price: Inexpensive
Area: Bruxelles, Centre-Ville, Dansaert
Address: Rue du Midi 45
1000 Brussels, Belgium
Phone: 02 511 35 45

#498
Chao Phraya
Cuisines: Thai
Average price: Expensive
Area: Ixelles, Bruxelles, La Bascule, Louise
Address: Avenue Louise 261
1000 Brussels, Belgium
Phone: 02 640 43 48

#499
Saudades do brasil
Cuisines: Brazilian
Average price: Expensive
Area: Bruxelles, Centre-Ville, Stalingrad
Address: Place vieille halle aux blés 30
1000 Brussels, Belgium
Phone: 02 503 04 97

#500
La Villa Lorraine
Cuisines: Belgian
Average price: Expensive
Area: Fort Jaco, Bruxelles, Bois de la Cambre
Address: Avenue du Vivier d'Oie 75
1000 Brussels, Belgium
Phone: 02 374 31 63

Made in the USA
Middletown, DE
27 December 2022

20520926R00029